The Triumph of Dionysos

Convivial processions, from antiquity to the present day

JOHN BOARDMAN

Archaeopress
2014

Archaeopress

Summertown Pavilion
18-24 Middle Way
Oxford OX2 7LG

www.archaeopress.com

ISBN 978 1 905739 70 7

© Archaeopress and J Boardman 2014

All rights reserved. No part of this book may be reproduced, stored in retrieval system, or transmitted, in any form or by any means, electronic, mechanical, photocopying or otherwise, without the prior written permission of the copyright owners.

CONTENTS

Preface   1

I. The Dionysiac Procession in Early Greece   3

II. The Egyptian Connection: staging the Triumph   10

III. Dionysos and Alexander the Great in the East   14

IV. The Procession in Hellenistic and Roman Art and Life   19

V. The Oriental Succession   45

VI. The Renaissance   50

VII. The Modern World   66

Abbreviations   78

Preface

The Greeks knew that their god Dionysos (Bacchus to the Romans) had conquered the whole world, to bring it the delights of wine, and that his greatest success had been in India. His victory procession back to Greece was a subject for artists and for real displays, which have provided models for triumphs, masques, civic and private celebrations, down to the present day. The model may be used to celebrate festivals for the gods, kings and emperors, successful athletes or sporting events, military victories, monumental entrance processions. The potential range of these and related celebrations is enormous, down to circus parades, the opening ceremonies for Olympic Games. For us the range will be more restricted, and often more serious, focusing on those involving wheeled vehicles of 'classical' type, and sometimes carrying images rather than 'real' gods, people or animals. The animals, especially the eastern, are important. The enthusiasm with which elements of the theme were accepted in the Renaissance may be exemplified by a famous ancient cameo in the Medici collection, an excerpt from the triumph [fig. 10], which Donatello adapted as a decorative marble roundel for the Farnese Palace in Florence [fig. 38], and the cameo reminds us of the sexual element – the acquisition of Ariadne by the god, which could be added to the general scenes of abandon in which a Pan or drunken old Silenos on a donkey was commonly also involved, as well as other heroes and divinities related to Dionysos either as drunkards or lovers.

Real chariots are the least important of the vehicles involved, since they can only hold one or two standing figures and are most appropriate for military triumphs. What was needed was transport which might accommodate several figures: commonly a low, flat four-wheeled cart, on which might be erected a tall platform for a throne, or a flatter chariot-type vehicle which could accommodate more than one figure if need be, even a boat on wheels, or what looks most like a Bath chair or a wheeled chaise-longue, like Donatello's, on which a couple can comfortably recline. Wild animals played a very important part in Dionysos' Indian triumph, with satyrs and wild women (his maenads, handling snakes), and especially wine. In antiquity such a celebration served as a model for the celebration of Alexander the Great's triumphs in the east, as well as those of Roman emperors, since the assimilation of a victor to a god was a practice encouraged by most rulers. Renaissance artists adopted the theme enthusiastically, mainly the theme of the god acquiring Ariadne on his return to Greece, and it has lived on as long as there has been a classical tradition in western art. The most distinguished latest contribution is by Salvador Dali [fig. 58], still dependent on the classical model, but we shall see that the procession itself and its classical elements have by no means been forgotten.

The account I give here has to be selective, but it concentrates on the classical renderings, their kin and succession, an art-historical exercise not unrelated to life. And it deals with Dionysos the easterner, not the northerner, who might be more relevant to many aspects of his cult, especially the mystic, but not to those aspects of his developing history which absorbed artists; nor whatever Mycenaean Greek figure bore his name on Linear B tablets; nor his many non-classical kin, like the Yoruba god Ogun and his phallic thyrsus;[1] nor the many parade vehicles of man's prehistory in which the sun disc or other symbols of the divine were carried in procession to entertain and reassure the populace; nor the very many religious or seasonal parades carrying icons or statues.[2] These are related only to the extent that long public parades are an ideal way to engage, entertain and even instruct the populace. I have not recorded my theme in a Dionysiac spirit, but the celebratory elements of it are exciting and inspirational, and if Dali is the best that can be mustered for the modern artist's reactions to the ancient images, at least something of the spirit of the live processions can be glimpsed in the circus parades with which this account closes.[3]

---

[1] W. Soyinka, *The Bacchae of Euripides* (1973) vi-vii.
[2] Well surveyed in Jennings, *Parades*.
[3] For an all-period bibliography of the subject of triumph see R. Baldwin, 'A Bibliography of the Literature on Triumph' in B. Wisch and S. Munshower (eds.), *Triumphal Celebrations and the Rituals of Statecraft* (1990) 358-385.

Chapter I

THE DIONYSIAC PROCESSION IN EARLY GREECE

We start soberly, to make a better acquaintance with our god as a serious actor in Greek religion as well as for his processional career. In the Ashmolean Museum at Oxford are fragments of a Greek black-figure clay vase found at Karnak in Egypt. One side depicts a big vine and vintage scene. The other side [fig. 1] can be restored as showing a large sailless boat (revealed by the scrap showing its boar's-head prow) being carried on the shoulders of men and attended by figures of satyrs – the animal-eared, tailed, phallos-waving attendants of Dionysos, one of them playing pipes. There can be little doubt that on the missing part of the boat (the majority) there was a figure of the god Dionysos himself, such as appears on later Attic scenes with the boat and satyrs [fig. 2]. There are much later references to a procession for Dionysos in which his priest steers a trireme boat carried to the agora of Smyrna,[1] and Smyrna or another East Greek city seems certainly the home of the artist who painted the Oxford vase soon after the middle of the sixth century BC. But there are no wheels here and we have to turn to Athens at the end of the century where we find on vases the Attic equivalent, also attested by texts, in which a figure of the god – most probably the priest dressed as the god – travels through the streets of Athens in a boat on wheels, attended by mock satyrs and music [fig. 2]. Attica too gives us more information about rustic Dionysiac processions, the *Dionysia in agrois*, involving the carriage of a massive phallos, which we see also on an Athenian vase, supported by a monster satyr.

---

[1] Philostratos, *Vit.soph*. i, 25.1.

Figure 1: East Greek black figure vase from Karnak, Egypt. Oxford, Ashmolean Museum 1924.264.

Figure 2: Attic black figure vase. London, British Museum B79.

The point of using a boat to celebrate the essentially agricultural and vinous, landlubber god Dionysos remains to be explained.[2] At any rate Dionysos was very addicted to wagons of some sort apart from those just mentioned; he would have appeared in the procession to any place where a Dionysiac theatrical production was to be staged, while on the stage itself there was on occasion the *ekkyklema*, a platform that could be wheeled out during or at the end of a play to display figures, even corpses, relevant to the action.[3]

Most of this is relatively early and in many ways very informal, but clearly such processions were a normal part of the religious life of Greek cities and villages, and especially in honour of Dionysos. Certainly there were other processions for deities at their sanctuaries. One of the more conspicuous was that in Athens for their goddess Athena. In the classical period the quadrennial Panathenaea festival featured a ship on wheels, carrying as its sail the peplos robe which was to be dedicated to the goddess on the Acropolis. The Spartans too were said to carry models of the rafts on which their Dorian ancestors entered the Peloponnese from the north, in their Karneia festival.[4] But we must return to Dionysos and our starting point in the vase found in Egypt.

Egypt will figure not a little in our narrative. At Karnak, the major royal and religious site, there was an annual festival (Opet) in which the boat of the sun god was carried in procession [cf. Fig. 3]. The presence of the Greek vase there can be no coincidence. The Greek who took it there, no doubt to dedicate, had seen the parallel with the local festival and may have especially ordered it at home, or at least chosen it as an appropriate special gift. It might even have been made in north Egypt where, it seems, Greek potter-painters were active in this period. But then the question arises whether the correspondence in

---

[2] A full account of the Karnak fragments and associations discussed in the following paragraphs, appears in my article 'A Greek Vase from Egypt', in *Journal of Hellenic Studies* 78 (1958) 4-12: the Karnak vase (Oxford 1924.264) – figs. 1-2, pl.1; the Attic ship on wheels (London B79)– fig. 3; the satyr and phallos (Florence 3897)– fig. 4. Further on Dionysos ship-cars, C. Auffarth, *Der drohende Untergang* (Berlin, 1991) 213-29; R. Parker, *Polytheism and Society at Athens* (Oxford, 2005) 302-3; *ThesCRA* V, 293 (the doubts about reconstruction are quite misplaced). The Egypt connection and the Karnak vase seem to be regularly omitted in recent discussions by historians of religion.

[3] On which see now J.D. Eis, *The Scene Wagon and the Ship of State* (New York, 2011).

[4] J. Boardman, *The Archaeology of Nostalgia* (2002) 85, and for other mythical ships. From the 1930s' excavations at the sanctuary of Apollo Phanaios in Chios there are unpublished (in Chios Museum) archaic fragments of clay models which vaguely resemble ship foreparts with roundels (wheels?) attached, and might be associated with ship processions of some sort.

practice was accidental. The fifth-century historian Herodotus (2. 48-9), who knew Egypt well, thought that the Dionysiac processions in Greece was derived from Egypt, including the carriage of cubit-high jointed images borne by women, with pipers, and that it was introduced in remote antiquity by Melampus ('black foot' – an African?), a seer who could talk to animals. Later, the historian Diodorus derived the Dionysiac phallos procession from Egypt too.[5] Another East-Greek-style vase found in Karnak, and of about the same date as the ship vase, has a satyr leading a large ram, a creature annually sacrificed there to Amun (= Greek Zeus), and so was perhaps also a deliberate choice for dedication.[6]

As for the ship on wheels, the Egyptian goddess Isis' ship is so depicted on a third-century AD painting in Ostia.[7]

We shall return to the Egyptian connection but should also consider other Greek processions of the archaic and classical periods, especially for any features which might relate to the later Dionysiac practices. Archaic depictions of chariot processions involving gods are plentiful in vase painting with a few on other monuments. The gods ride and are often accompanied on foot by other deities. Mortal rustic, marital and other processions are commonly on foot, accompanied by music and often dancing. Dionysiac ones generally seem to be given a mythological setting and describe the Return of Hephaistos to Olympus, whence the god had been thrown for binding Hera to her throne, and the god is often depicted lame from the fall. He is accompanied by Dionysos, another 'lame' god, with his full rout of satyrs and maenads, music and dancing, but for transport nothing more than an ass.

This is the sort of mythical processional occasion which could easily, through art, have provided a model for real rustic celebrations of the god and wine.

The use of a chariot, however, is most relevant. The chariot was not a weapon of war for Greeks of this period, but it was used for racing in the Games (themselves very religious occasions) and ceremonially, being especially associated with heroes and a major feature in the Homeric epic poems about the war at Troy. Most of the gods were at times represented in chariots, often attended by other gods. There may, however, on occasion

---

[5] Herodotus 2, 48-9; Diodorus 1.22.7.
[6] *Journal of Hellenic Studies* 78 (1958) pl. 2b.
[7] *ThesCRA* VII 234, pl. 31.1. I do not think the Late Dynastic model of a Mediterranean-type ship on wheels found in Gurob (Nile delta) can be easily accommodated in the Dionysos-Egypt story: S. Wachsmann, *Gurob ship-cart model and its Mediterranean context* (Texas, 2012), especially ch. 2, but it might be borne in mind.

be a mortal association also in the divine chariot scenes. When the tyrant Peisistratos marched to take over Athens in about 560 BC he came in a chariot (not, as we have seen, a war chariot so much as a parade chariot) in the company of a woman who had been dressed up as the city goddess Athena. There is good if indirect evidence even in the earlier archaic period that prominent mortals could be assimilated to gods or heroes in popular ideology and art if not religion. In Athens Herakles, then Theseus, were the prominent heroes, and closely associated with politicians of the day. It was soon to become a very common practice, especially in the Hellenistic period, starting with Alexander 'the Great' who could be assimilated to a Zeus, Herakles or Dionysos. Athena's own procession at the Panathenaea festival in Athens has been noted already for its inclusion of a ship on wheels, but most of it passed through Athens on foot or on horseback, the Acropolis being inaccessible to chariots. The carriage of gods' statues on chariots was probably commonplace – thus, there is record for that of Dionysos being so treated on early third-century BC Delos,[8] and this was a feature of the spring Dionysia festival in Attica. Even eighth-century BC Greece may have had a statue-in-chariot tradition, in Crete, with a nature goddess, shown on a vase.[9]

Egypt requires special attention not only for this early period but also for developments in the post-Alexander, Hellenistic (Ptolemaic) period from the late fourth century BC on. Processions were an important part of rituals both for the gods and for the dead. Boats figure prominently, both because of the simple presence of the Nile and for its special function at Karnak as being the divider between the lands of the living and the dead (on the west bank). Images of the dead, of kings and of gods, were carried on boats on various occasions, often accommodated in individual shrines. The boat itself is normally carried on the shoulders of men [fig. 3], as on the Oxford vase, but could also be moved on sledges and pulled by oxen. Wheeled vehicles, normal in the Greek world, were less important in a land dominated by its river and relatively roadless, and Egyptian war chariots were fast and flimsy. For our purposes it is the Egyptian practice that must have been the most influential, but the notion of carrying statues of divinities, either for ritual or between cities, was known too in early Mesopotamia and is virtually universal.

A god's statue in its way signified the independence and power of a city, so that its theft was a matter of some concern. Whence the significance of the 'Palladion' statue of Athena at Troy which, once stolen by the Greeks,

---

[8] *Inscriptiones Graecae* XI.2, 158A.70, 161A.90-1; T. Homolle, *Bulletin de Correspondance Hellénique* 14 (1890) 503-4.
[9] *ThesCRA* II.5, 482, no. 583 (fig.). Ibid., 477-488 on the carriage of cult statues (C. Lochin).

Figure 3: Relief at Karnak, Egypt.

spelled the downfall of the city. Later and elsewhere there are the great Krishna processions of divine statues on chariots, and the Juggernaut, and much more.

For the early period we have seen that a Greece-Egypt parallel can be found. Whether it is significant or not is another matter. A boat is a less obvious vehicle for Dionysos, a rustic god, than for the gods and divine kings along the Nile. The Athenian Exekias' famous cup of about 530 BC shows the god alone on a ship, its mast growing a vine, and dolphins around [fig. 4].[10] One explanation is that he is bringing the gift of the vine and wine from Naxos to Athens. He was said also to have sailed west where he was attacked by Tyrrhenian (Etruscan) pirates whom he turned into dolphins. The story appears in the Hesiodic Hymn to Dionysos, of uncertain date, but possibly archaic, 6th-century. The subject appears quite explicitly on the Lysicrates Monument in Athens in the 4th century BC, without any ships.[11] Whether such stories are enough to justify a Dionysiac ship procession, in Athens and East Greece, is not clear; otherwise we might have to judge that observation

---

[10] J. Boardman, *Athenian Black Figure Vases* (1974, 1991) fig. 104 (Munich 2044).
[11] J. Boardman, *Greek Sculpture; the Late Classical Period* (1995) fig. 16.

Figure 4: Attic black figure vase. Munich 2044.

of what were taken to be Dionysiac practices in Egypt suggested that for the image of the Greek god too a ship could be appropriate and serve as a carriage. We would expect to see it first in East Greece (and we do, on the Karnak vase which is of East Greek parentage) but Athens' later adoption of the motif and with a wheeled ship is at least odd, and the connotation there seems more rustic (a spring festival) than maritime.[12] Maybe the maritime associations of Dionysos have older roots, and we need to look again at Egypt.

---

[12] *LIMC* III, Dionysos nos. 788-90, 792, 827-9. For the Exekias vase and full discussion of the subject see now E.A. Mackay, *Tradition and Originality: A Study of Exekias* (Oxford, BAR 2092, 2010) 221-241.

Chapter II

THE EGYPTIAN CONNECTION: STAGING THE TRIUMPH

The Egyptian connection becomes perhaps more important for our main theme in the Hellenistic period, after the foundation of Alexandria and Greek artists' more immediate exposure to Egyptian religious art and behaviour. Egypt had become part of the great Persian Empire, and so was in due course invaded and taken by the Macedonian Alexander in the later fourth century BC. The Greek connection was an old one – they had sought trade there and founded a trading town (Naucratis) in the Nile delta before 600 BC, and they had served as mercenaries for Egyptian kings.

Hellenistic Alexandria developed a more strongly Greek aspect than hitherto, as a source for trade and for study by Greek authors (with its great Library), as well as being a centre for the development of peculiarly 'Alexandrian' Greek Hellenistic arts which were widely influential. A reflection of this is strongest in the account of a famous procession mounted for King Ptolemy Philadelphos II (who was not, of course, an Egyptian by birth, nor Greek, but Macedonian) in Alexandria in the late 270s BC. It probably celebrated a 'Ptolemieia' festival in honour of the royal family, including images of royalty and the Greek gods, and especially a section devoted to Dionysos. The Macedonian element and reference to Alexander and his equation with the god Dionysos, especially à propos of his 'return' from India, mean that I here anticipate what will later be discussed about Alexander in the east, but in this context it is the 'heritage' of comparable Egyptian royal and divine processions that is equally at issue. I think it difficult to believe that the procession took the form it did without consciously imitating current or recent Egyptian practices.

It certainly goes far beyond what we know of any earlier Greek processions for gods or mortals, and its designers and sponsors in Alexandria must have been well aware of Egyptian practice and inspired by it, no doubt also exploiting Egyptian expertise in such matters.

The procession was described by Kallixeinos of Rhodes in a book about Alexandria. His exact dates are uncertain and the text of his description of the procession is preserved only in a long quotation by Athenaios of Naucratis (in Egypt) who dates the event to the reign of Ptolemy Philadelphos II, and was himself writing in about AD 200. We cannot know whether Kallixeinos himself saw the procession; most probably not, and scholars believe that he wrote much later but from detailed records. His description has been carefully and fully discussed by Ellen Rice in a book of 1983.[1] As described, the procession in many ways beggars belief for its complexity and size, and some scholars have questioned its authenticity as a description of an actual event. Dr Rice effectively dispels such doubts, and when we add the probability that Egypt itself provided the model for much of what was included, we need not even think that some aspects were exaggerated. It gives every appearance of being based on an official record of what had taken place, if not eye-witness. It also helps explain much of the contemporary and later history of depictions of Dionysiac processions in the Alexandrian and Hellenistic Greek worlds, which is our main theme.

I summarise the description considerably here. The procession started from a massive pavilion-marquee. It was led by parades displaying personifications of the Morning and Evening Stars, with parts devoted to the parents of the Egyptian kings and to the Greek gods and their attributes. The Dionysiac section followed, attended by men dressed as satyrs, and women as Victories with golden wings carrying nine-feet-high incense burners; then a double altar nine-feet long, and boys with incense in 120 trenchers, and more satyrs with golden crowns; personifications of the Year, the Penteteris (five-year festival – personified as a beautiful woman), more satyrs, a priest of Dionysos and Delphic tripods up to 18-feet tall. Then came the carts, a four-wheeler 21-feet long drawn by 180 men carrying a 15-foot statue of Dionysos pouring a libation, with a crater and table before him, in a canopy adorned with flowers and masks; then priests and women imitating maenads, some with daggers, some with snakes. The next cart, led by 60 men, carried a statue of Nysa

---

[1] E.E. Rice, *The Grand Procession of Ptolemy Philadelphus* (Oxford, 1983). And see P.M. Fraser, *Ptolemaic Alexandria* (Oxford, 1972) I, 202-7, for an assessment of the Dionysiac/Ptolemaic associations. On the pavilion (Athen. 196a-197c) see E. Calandra, 'The Ephemeral and the Eternal' in *Archeologia, Anthropologia, Storia* (Athens, 2011) – review, *Rev. Arch.* 2013, 416-8.

(Dionysos' nurse, but also an eastern location as we shall see), an automaton which could stand up and pour a libation mechanically. (Recall the 'jointed' figures recorded for earlier Greek rustic processions.) Then a 30x24-foot cart pulled by 300 men and a wine press with 60 satyrs; another with 600 men carrying a massive flask holding 3000 measures of wine. Then more satyrs with precious vessels and a silver crater holding 600 measures, on a cart, with figure decoration, more vessels and furniture, gold plate and wine presses. 1600 boys with pitchers and jars of sweetmeats, then 6-foot tables with figure tableaux. A 33x21-foot cart carried a cave with springs of milk and wine and figures of the god Hermes with Nymphs (a popular Hellenistic motif for votive reliefs). Another carried a tableau of the 'Return of Dionysos from India' with an 18-foot statue of the god lying on an elephant, attended by a 7-foot satyr, followed by a long procession including wild animals and precious objects, as booty.[2] Another four-wheeler had a different Dionysos tableau, the god fleeing from Hera. Then come statues of Alexander and Ptolemy with the city of Corinth and women representing other Greek cities. One cart carried a 135-foot long thyrsos (the Dionysiac wand, essentially a fennel stalk with vines) and others statues of kings and gods followed by a massive band of musicians and golden-horned bulls. Finally, the gods are again honoured, as is Alexander himself, whose golden statue was set on a chariot drawn by four real elephants, with Victory and Athena; royal thrones and displays of sheer golden wealth. At the end – regiments of the army, infantry and cavalry.

Even this very compressed account of the procession may arouse an element of doubt in the mind of the reader, but all parts of it are quite plausible and some details, even the trivial, ring true of what was possible and practised in Hellenistic Alexandria, and Egypt generally, including even the automaton statue and the size of the figures. Antiquity could think at least as big as any modern impresario, and we are in the land of the Pyramids, the great Lighthouse of Alexandria, and truly monumental sculpture. The way gods were presented in the Egyptian manner, like the Dionysos under a canopy, might well also have come to influence the way they were soon depicted in other Alexandrian arts, notably on cameos. The scale is colossal, but so was that of many well-attested later triumphs in the Greek and Roman world, and at Alexandria the Ptolemies, who regarded themselves as gods, had the model of an Egypt long used to processions of comparable luxury, magnitude and content, with the carriage of statues and groups. Add that Alexander's taste

---

[2] The list of animals is worth detailing since there will be later echoes: 130 Ethiopian sheep, 300 Arabian, 20 Euboean, 26 Indian white zebus, 8 Ethiopian, a she-bear, 14 leopards, 16 civet-cats, 4 lynxes, 3 bear cubs, one giraffe, one Ethiopian rhinoceros.

of the orient had also taught Macedonians how to be ambitious in matters other than the purely military.

The glorious display in Alexandria was by no means the end of the matter. We shall have occasion later to see how it related to Roman ideas about how to conduct a Triumph, but there is another display, roughly rivalling the Alexandrian and not much discussed, but also Macedonian (Seleucid not Ptolemaic) in inspiration and taking place closer to Alexander's route – at Daphne, near Antioch in Syria, in 166/5 BC. It was staged by Antiochus IV, who had himself recently invaded Egypt and had to confront the Romans. His month-long celebration involved games, gladiators and wild-beast fights, but the centrepiece was a great procession which, in Polybius' account (30.25.2-26.4), is strongly reminiscent of Alexandria. It was more military, and of the 10,000 soldiers half had golden shields, a quarter bronze, a quarter silver. More to the point were the hundred elephant chariots and 36 more with 'housings', i.e. battle-howdahs. But there was a strong civilian and religious (Greek) element: 'For representations of all the gods and spirits mentioned or worshipped by men and of all the heroes were carried along…all accompanied by representations executed in precious materials of the myths relating to them.' There were quantities of gold and silver plate, none weighing less than a thousand drachmae. Nothing more specifically Dionysiac is mentioned (except that the private secretary involved was called Dionysios), but by this date and in this location the model must have been clear, and it was a positive challenge to the shows devised by both the Romans in Macedonia and the Egyptians.

Chapter III

DIONYSOS AND ALEXANDER THE GREAT IN THE EAST

We retrace our steps. In his play, the Bacchae, first performed in Athens, probably in 406 BC soon after his death, the poet Euripides lets Dionysos dwell on his journeys. He places his home in Anatolia (Turkey), with the Lydians and Phrygians, but lets him roam the high plains of Persia, the walled towns of Bactria (north Afghanistan), bleak Media (north Persia), rich Arabia; and, he says, he set 'Asia' dancing, before turning to the first (for him) of the Greek cities, Thebes (lines 13-22). This is in keeping with Hesiod's Hymn to Dionysos. In it 'the father of man and gods (Zeus) bore him (Dionysos) far from men, hiding the event from white-armed Hera. There is a high mountain, Nysa, rich in woods, far away in Phoenicia near the waters of Egypt' (lines 1-9). Geographically, all this means is 'somewhere far off to the east'.

Dionysos was always an uneasy 'Olympian', although he was accepted into the canonic treatment of the family of the gods. But he could be seen also as a far more universal figure, and various authors had him as conqueror of most parts of the known world. Diodorus Siculus (3.63) has the most ancient Dionysos as an Indian, and writes (3.66, 68-70) of his birth in a distant Nysa; and as a conqueror, not only a soldier, but as promoter of the vine and a way of life in which ecstasy and the irrational had major parts to play, a role readily abetted by the effects of wine, I am told.

The god's conventional military capabilities were otherwise only called into play in the part he played in the Gods' war against the Giants, a subject for Greek art from early times.

Figure 5: Attic red figure vase. Paris, Louvre MNB 1036.

He generally fights on foot, helped by his troop of maenads and satyrs and various animals.[1]

He had occupied a chariot earlier, as might any Olympian, as we have seen, but in the 4th century begin scenes of him in animal chariots, with panthers, griffins, goats and the like, and we seem to be approaching new and more exotic attitudes to the god, admitting oriental associations, and once at least he seems most like a young warrior, threatening, his spear a thyrsos wand, his team a panther, griffin and bull [fig. 5].[2] On a Boeotian vase his chariot is drawn by donkeys and has protruding from it a great phallos (with a sea-monster's head) [fig. 6].[3] All this contributes to his universal, not-quite-Olympian image.

A far more explicit reference to the god in the east is offered in the scene on an Athenian red-figure vase of around 400 BC [fig. 7].[4] The god (it is surely

---

[1] For Dionysos in the battle of Gods and Giants see F. Lissarrague in *Images et Société en Grèce Ancienne: Cahiers d'Archéologie Romande* 36 (Lausanne, 1987) 111-120.
[2] *LIMC* III, pl. 353, Dionysos 461 (Paris MNB 1036); ibid. p. 463 for others.
[3] *LIMC* VIII, pl. 500, Ketos 40 (Mainz). F. Brommer wonders whether it is Boeotian: *Archäologischer Anzeiger* 1985, 25-7.
[4] London E 695; Furtwängler-Reichhold, *Griechische Vasenmalerei* II (Munich, 1904-32) pl.

Figure 6: Boeotian red figure vase, Mainz.

he), dressed like a Persian, is sitting side-saddle on a Bactrian two-humped camel. Around him men and girls are dancing, also dressed as orientals, with kithara, tambourine, torch, fan and lyre, while at the sides two Persians dance in their familiar native, spinning style with hands clasped over their heads, the first 'whirling dervishes'.

The camel type itself is an indication of Greek awareness of Asian lands. In the mid-6th century an East Greek vase showed a Bactrian camel being led by a hairy, tailless satyr.[5] The Persian Dionysos belongs to a period in which many Persian subjects appear in Greek art, since the former enemy had become, for some, an ally, for some, a source of finance, for many a not wholly objectionable overlord. Moreover, The Persians had a reputation for their fondness for wine and were said to prefer to take decisions when drunk, not sober.[6]

78.3.
[5] J. Boardman, *Early Greek Vase Painting* (London, 1998) fig. 350, from Old Smyrna.
[6] Athenaeus 10.434. Herodotus 1.133. T. Daryaea in *Iranian Language and Culture* (Essays, Gernot Ludwig Windfuhr; Mazda, 2012) 28-43, on Persians and wine.

Figure 7: Attic red figure vase. London, British Museum E 695.

The anecdotes about Dionysos in the east also occur in narratives about Alexander the Great, whose invasion of Persia took him yet farther east into Central Asia and lands also ruled by the Persians. Here the men of Nysa begged him to spare them because, after defeating the Indians, the god Dionysos had founded their city as a monument to his victory (just as Alexander himself founded several Alexandrias, besides the one in Egypt), the town being named for his nurse Nysa, and with the nearby mountain Meros (see below); and 'nowhere else in India does the ivy grow' (Arrian, *Exp.* 5.1.5; *Ind.* 5.8,9). It is thanks to Dionysos that the Indians are so fond of music and dancing (Arrian, *Exp.* 6.3.5) and they wear 'the dappled costume like *bacchoi* of Dionysos'.

There was even a story (sensibly disbelieved by Arrian, *Exp.* 6.28.1) that on his march home through Carmania (south Persia) Alexander himself rode in two chariots, with music, jollity and extravagance, copying the god's procession home.[7] At best, they may have managed a party (*komos*) and a

---

[7] On this non-event see A.B. Bosworth, *From Arrian to Alexander* (Oxford, 1988) 66-9.

later celebration in Persia of a Dionysos festival,[8] not long before his death in Babylon. The Indians said that the god made one Spatemba king of India, and his son was the Buddha (Arrian, *Ind.* 8,1; and 9.9-11, for other Indian views on their Dionysian past).

So the Alexander-Dionysos connection is well attested, and the Macedonian was not slow to encourage association with Greek heroes: Herakles (who also had an eastern record) and even gods (Zeus Ammon in Egypt). There was little trouble in antiquity in creating genealogies for kings to give them divine ancestors, and the assimilation of a political leader to a hero or god had begun in the archaic period and became a commonplace in the Hellenistic. Macedonian Alexander was anxious to strengthen his links with Greek tradition, however scornful he may have been of most contemporary Greeks. His march against Persia was allegedly retribution for the Persian sack of Athens in the early 5th century BC, carrying out what his father Philip II had intended. Essentially, both were intent on expansion of power on whatever pretext, and Philip had soundly beaten dissenting Greeks on the field of battle at Chaironeia in central Greece in 338 BC, ending for good Greek hopes of any sort of unity and independence, while Alexander destroyed Thebes. So much for 'champions of Greece'.

Dionysos' eastern adventures strengthened the link with Alexander, which is why the god's Indian triumph was included in the Ptolemaic procession described above, and in many later. Nysa, whether a nurse or a location, was located by Alexander's expedition in the Gandhara area, and a hill called Meros (Greek for 'thigh'; the god was thought to have been born from Zeus' thigh), appropriately covered with vines, while some scholarly erudition was expended on tracing other locations on Alexander's progress through Asia that had, or could be made to seem to have, associations with the wine god. It has indeed been argued that Alexander, as 'King of Asia', was consciously claiming a Dionysiac heritage, if not even paternity, and that the diadem which he adopted and was to be taken as the badge of Macedonian kingship, was Dionysos' own.[9] Thus myth, history, religion, geography, and Alexander's pretensions as god and success as conqueror, conspired to create a pseudo-historical event that would haunt western art for centuries to come.

---

[8] Thus, P. Goukowsky, *Alexandre et Dionysos* (Nancy, 1981) ch. 4, and for earlier associations.
[9] R.R.R. Smith, *Hellenistic Royal Portraits* (Oxford, 1988) 34-8; E.A. Fredricksmeyer in *Trans. Amer.Phil.Soc.* 127 (1997) 97-109; if not the Persian Great King's ribbon: R. Lane Fox, in C. Tuplin (ed.), *Persian Responses* (Oxford, BAR, 2007) 278; but then one might have expected the Persian crown too: Alexander was ready to 'dress oriental' on occasion. Cf. B.M. Kingsley on the kausia and diadem, *American Journal of Archaeology* 88 (1984) 66-8.

Chapter IV

THE PROCESSION IN HELLENISTIC AND ROMAN ART AND LIFE

The new subject for Greek and Roman artists was expressed especially in two media: on cameos of the later Hellenistic and early Roman period (second century BC to first AD); and on stone sarcophagi mainly of the second and third centuries AD. The Hellenistic interest derives from Alexandrian Egypt, as has been shown. The Roman has a different history under the empire, more involved with politics, since Greek Dionysos gets associated with the wrong people and has soon to be displaced by the Italian god Saturn, though not for long. To the Romans Dionysos was Bacchus, but I do not here change his name, except for the occasional 'bacchic' or 'bacchant' (Greek 'maenad').

Of Roman individuals who claimed an affinity with the god Mark Antony is prominent. He was closely associated with Greece and Alexandria (thanks to Cleopatra) and campaigned in the east. He had already adopted a Dionysiac personality and identity when in Greece with his Roman wife Octavia in 39/38 BC. On his arrival at Ephesus he was greeted by 'bacchants' and boys dressed as satyrs and Pans, while the city was festooned with ivy and thyrsoi, and echoed to harps, pipes and flutes. Antony did march east through Parthia intending to attack the Indians. He never made it, and returned to Cleopatra, but he brought back with him the captured Armenian king Artavasdes in 34 BC, and had a triumphal procession where he presided as a 'New Dionysos', in its way an echo of the great Ptolemaic procession of the 270s BC.

This may, with Alexander's heritage, have also contributed to Ptolemy XII's (reigned 80-58 and 55-1 BC) adoption of the title Neos Dionysos. Alexandria plays a major role in this story for its festive record:

> and the Alexandrians rushed to the festival,
> filled with excitement, and shouted acclaim
> in Greek, and in Egyptian, and some in Hebrew,
> enchanted by the lovely spectacle –
> though of course they knew what they were worth,
> what empty words these kingdoms were.
>
> (C.P. Cavafy, 'Alexandrian Kings', trans. D. Mendelson)

Antony and Cleopatra posed for artists as Dionysos or Osiris, and as Selene (the moon goddess) or Isis,[1] and conducted themselves as such at the great 'Donations' celebration of 34 BC, when their eastern empire was distributed.[2]

Antony had other Dionysiac qualities, as a lion-tamer. Lions had been becoming familiar in Rome, at Games and for display. Mark Antony was alleged to be the first who successfully harnessed them to a chariot.[3] In art this is celebrated by a bronze group made in 1898 by Arthur Strasser, which stood in Paris, and now before the Secession Building in Vienna [fig. 8], but not in antiquity. Eventually it became clear that the god had deserted Antony. After

Figure 8: Bronze group by Arthur Strasser. Vienna.

---

[1] Dio Cassius 50.5.3 and 25.4.
[2] P.J. Jones, *Cleopatra. The Last Pharaoh* (Oklahoma, 2006) 32-9.
[3] Antony as Dionysos, see Pliny 8,21,55 (lions); Plutarch, *Antony* 9 (lions), 24.3 (Ephesus), 37.4 (India), 60.3 ('new Dionysos'), 75.3-4 (deserted); Dio Cassius 48.39.2, 49.40.3-41.3,

Figure 9: Bronze sestertius of Titus.

Antony's defeat at Actium official Rome – Octavian, the future Emperor Augustus, who had once himself been associated with Dionysos (Antony becoming then a 'false Dionysos')[4] – came to prefer the Roman/Italian gods, such as Apollo or Saturn, as the inspiration for Roman culture and success, so that Rome for a while turned its back on imperial Dionysiac fantasies.[5]

Nevertheless, the emperor Titus rides high behind an elephant team on a coin (*sestertius*) of AD 80-1 [fig. 9],[6] and we shall shortly have to consider the relationship of the tradition of our scenes to those of the formal Roman Triumph. But, in the first and second centuries AD, generally only deified Roman emperors are accorded an elephant chariot,[7] and with this we turn from history and myth to art.[8]

---

[4] J.A. Stevens, *Phoenix* 53 (1999) 288-90; reflected in the poet Horace.
[5] Well explored by A.-F. Jaccottet in *Festrituale in der römischen Kaiserzeit* (ed. J. Rüpke, Tübingen, 2008) 201-13.
[6] *American Journal of Archaeology* 114 (2010), 48, fig. 3, and 46-8 for *carpenta* carriages.
[7] K.W.Harl, *Civic Coins and Civic Politics in the Roman Empire AD 180-275* (Berkeley, 1987) 48, pl. 18.3; pl. 35.8,9 for the god in elephant and panther chariots. For medallions of Hadrian and Antoninus Pius with Dionysiac chariots see Matz I, Beil. 1a-e.
[8] On animals in Roman circuses and triumphs see also the epigrams in 'Martial' *de spectaculis libellus*.

Figure 10: Cameo. Medici Collection, Florence.

Cameos

Cameos – semi-precious stones cut in relief, generally for setting in finger-rings but sometimes larger, seem to have been invented as a new genre for the jeweller (already used as relief work on some gems) in the 2nd or possibly 3rd century BC, and very probably in Alexandria. The range of subjects did not altogether duplicate that for engraved gems (intaglios) and, since the cameos were more display pieces and much worn by women, there was a tendency towards subjects involving women and Aphrodite, Eros and the like. As gifts they also had a certain propaganda value – they were far more easily viewable than intaglios and therefore attracted portraits.

The popularity of Dionysiac subjects might in part have been a product of their popularity in Alexandria, but these subjects soon spread through the whole Greek and late Republican/early Imperial Roman world. Dating them is not easy, and most that are presented here, to display the range of subjects, probably belong to the first centuries BC/AD. A tiny cameo, of course, cannot present a whole procession, only individual elements, notably the vehicle carrying the god or his consort or servants, but some are quite populous.

Two pieces especially display the elements in such scenes which remain prominent throughout antiquity and were much copied later. One is the

Figure 11: Cameo. Medici Collection, Florence.   *Figure 12: Glass cameo. London, Walters no. 3856.*

Medici cameo copied by Donatello; the other is a glass cameo in the British Museum which is an ancient cast of a very fine stone original – not an uncommon procedure in this period.

The Medici cameo [fig. 10] must have been found in Italy to reach the great collection in Florence.[9] It shows the vehicle as a wheeled chaise-longue holding a youthful and part-dressed Dionysos, attended by a satyr who stands on the ground beyond, a support position sometimes adopted by other figures in such scenes. It is pulled by two women with butterfly wings, like Psychai (personification of the Soul and Eros/Cupid's consort), one of whom looks round at the other. Oddly, one has heart-shaped wings (no doubt Psyche herself), the other straight wings and wild hair, a distinction yet to be explained, if indeed it is significant. A similar pair but both with straight wings, led by an Eros, pull a simple chariot holding Ariadne with a thyrsos and another Eros [fig. 11].[10] Other attendants are, as often, Erotes. One on the Medici cameo is active, as we shall find many others in such scenes, pushing at the wheel. The other, hardly less characteristically as we

---

[9] Vollenweider, *Steinschneidekunst* pl. 23.1. Donatello turns the near-naked Dionysos into a dressed woman, attended by a youth; see E. Simon, in *Schriften zur Kunstgeschichte* (Stuttgart, 2003) 85. A 16th-century Medici copy has a half-naked Ariadne with a satyr (*Pitti* Cat.6, no. 9).

[10] A. Giuliano, *I Cammei della Collezione Medicea* (1989) no.57. They appear alone on the cameo: M.L. Vollenweider, *Deliciae Leonis* (1964) no. 93, where there is also a good discussion of the group.

Figure 13: Cameo. Paris, Cab.Med., Chab. 61.

shall see, stands on the chariot pole holding up a torch horizontally, rather like a spear.

On the glass cameo [fig. 12] (which must be an ancient cast copy of a stone cameo)[11] the vehicle is a flat two-wheeled cart carrying a throne on which is seated Ariadne with a youthful Dionysos in her lap, both barely clothed. Behind them a small Psyche plays Pan-pipes, in front, apparently stepping on to the cart pole, is an Eros holding up what is surely a torch. The team pulling the cart is another Psyche figure, and a young satyr, both looking round. Over the break in front of them is the head of a Pan who is probably part of the team. Overhead an Eros flies holding a long scarf. Below the groundline are a rosette, flower, and ribbon.

There are many variants or simplifications of these basic scenes, some simply omitting some of the figures, since the glass cameo is certainly the most populous. Overall, one may say that the obvious attentions of Erotes, satyrs and sometimes maenads are commonplace, that of Pan less common. The traction need not be by humanoids, but by centaurs or felines, the latter especially reminiscent of the Indian triumph. But the triumph, when both

---

[11] London, Walters no. 3856; Vollenweider, *Steinschneidekunst* pl. 24.5 (as Venus and Adonis, presumably because the woman seems the senior figure).

Figure 14: Cameo, Naples, Mus.Naz.

Figure 15: Cameo, London, Walters no. 3488.

Dionysos and Ariadne appear, is also in some respects a marriage procession, although Ariadne is present also in many of the eastern scenes, and it seems likely that the story was that the god picked up Ariadne (who had been abandoned by Theseus on Naxos) at the end of his journey back to Greece.

To look at variants: on a cameo in Paris [fig. 13] the traction is by two centaurs, male and female, playing cymbals and a lyre. One Eros with a torch leads, another wraps Dionysos and Ariadne in a scarf, and the god, with a thyrsos, is seated in her lap, as on the glass cameo [fig. 12], while the mount too is a flat platform carrying a throne. There are marine figures below.[12] For the centaurs there is also a St Petersburg cameo, a male and a female with a tambourine, and Dionysos seated on the chariot as on a throne.[13] Also a fine Naples fragment with the same centaurs, but a young male for the woman, and pouring into a cup [fig. 14].[14] A cameo in New York has the couple on the cart as [fig. 12] but with the Eros with raised torch standing on the back

---

[12] Cab.Med., Chabouillet no. 61. G.M.A. Richter, *The Engraved Gems of the Romans* (London, 1971) no. 165. *LIMC* III, Dionysos/Bacchus no. 215, pl. 450

[13] Vollenweider, *Steinschneidekunst*, pl. 23.5,7.

[14] Ibid., pl. 23. 2,6.

of two panthers.[15] Two lions (male and female?) also pull the chariot or cart (missing) on a fine cameo fragment in London signed by Sostratos, where they are being led by an Eros. I show [fig. 15] the full scene as it appears on another London cameo.[16] This is going to be an inspirational group. Eros rather steals these scenes which are as much nuptial as they are triumphal.

Other 'minor arts' contribute something to our evidence for the use of elaborate processional equipment in Roman public life, in their details probably owing much to the inspiration of the popular Dionysiac procession. Coin devices are a major source.

Noble women were carried in *carpenta*, which are covered wagons drawn by horses, but males, emperors, may have an elephant chariot, and are placed on thrones set high on a base on a flat cart. This implies their deification and is a type which may derive from Egypt, but which certainly belongs also to the more usual Roman triumphal processions, where the victor is in a chariot or seated high for visibility, and it plays its part in later presentations of the Dionysiac processions.

Sarcophagi

Before we turn to representations on sarcophagi a word must be said about the relationship between our Dionysiac processions and the Roman Triumph.[17] A military triumph is a matter for war chariots, display by the victor and his troops, and display of the defeated in person and in terms of spoils of war. In Rome such triumphs were massive and spectacular, but it seems likely that they may have borrowed from the Alexandrian Greek representations and even the tradition of the Dionysiac processions, themselves triumphal to the extent that the god was thought to have conquered the east, fighting is sometimes shown, and the fact that the paradigm was Alexander's military feats, partly matched in the east by Romans. The Roman general Pompey's

---

[15] G.M.A. Richter, *Catalogue of Engraved Gems* (New York, 1936) no. 617.

[16] Sostratos – Vollenweider, *Steinschneidekunst* pl. 24.1-3; Walters, no. 3462, pl. 34. Our fig. 15 is ibid. no. 3488, pl. 34.

[17] Explored by M. Beard in *The Roman Triumph* (Harvard, 2007), esp. pp. 315-8. She is unduly sceptical of the veracity of the description of the Alexandria festival by Euxeinos (pp. 168-9), and ignores that of Antiochus at Antioch (not, of course, Roman). A. Erskine expresses reservations about associating Hellenistic parades with Roman triumphs in *Rituals of Triumph in the Mediterranean World* (ed. T. Schneider, Leiden, 2013) 37-56. Also, R.A. Hazzard, *Imagination of a Monarchy; Studies in Ptolemaic Propoaganda* (Toronto, 2000; *Phoenix* Suppl. 37) ch.4. Most fully on Roman Triumphs, I. Ostenberg, *Staging the World* (Lund, 2003).

triumph of 61 BC[18] is a good case. He had defeated the Persian King Mithradates of Pontos, who was a champion of the Greeks and had sought to keep the Romans away from Greece and the east, starting by massacring all the Romans in Anatolia. He had allied himself with and led Parthians/Persians, so the parallel was apt, and several elements in it echo the Ptolemaic procession at Alexandria – conspicuous displays of money and wealth, carrying Mithradates' throne, his sceptre and his gold statue eight cubits tall, a golden mountain with vines (recalling mount Meros), massive metal vessels, 'images' of the defeated kings. In his chariot Pompey himself wore a cloak that had, allegedly, once belonged to Alexander. For his African triumphs he included elephants, as had Marcellus for a Punic defeat in 211 BC (Livy 26.21.9). There is enough here to suggest that no little was modelled on Alexander/Dionysos processions in the Greek world and Alexandria, though the Greek god never soiled his hands with weaponry (there are late exceptions). Later, as we shall see, there was a return influence on the depictions of Dionysiac triumphal processions. The type of carriage with the god/victor seated high and alone, which we have just visited, is clearly one which is appropriate to a mortal triumph in which the victor is prominently displayed. Otherwise, what we can learn of the trappings of a mortal Triumph only superficially reproduce those of the divine.

This too should be the place at which to point out that the Dionysiac scenes in later art may not easily identify themselves as specific moments in the story. For some authors Dionysos' military campaigns involved the forcible coercion of the whole world to his vinous culture. This, and the initial move against the east, is probably not to be distinguished in art. The actual fighting against the Indians is rare; more common is the immediate aftermath with captured Indians, followed by the triumphal return, whether en route or on arrival home. But excerpts are common and his triumph affects almost all representations of the god for the rest of antiquity, and beyond, helped by the various enactments of it in a context of mortal triumphs and of mortal aspirations to divinity. And we may suspect that his discovery of Ariadne, as an important episode on the homecoming, may have been of some importance, as it certainly was in later centuries when the romantic element was more greatly appreciated.

---

[18] Beard, op.cit., 9-18.

The relevant scenes on Roman sarcophagi[19] are of the second half of the second century AD and first quarter of the third. From the late first century on sarcophagi had been decorated with relief scenes of mythical content, whether or not obviously associated with ideas of immortality or even of an afterlife. Dionysiac subjects had been common enough, with themes of initiation and celebration prominent, but this concentration on the processions should be explicable. In the years about 160-180 AD (the reign of Marcus Aurelius) there are some scenes which seem specifically of the god's march on India and, unusually, fighting there. By that time the Parthians had moved into Armenia and defeated Roman armies, eventually avenged, and Mesopotamia had fallen under the 'protection' of Rome. Perhaps these eastern military episodes were enough to reawaken parallels with Dionysos' eastern expedition, and not without recollection of Alexander's. The emperor and his son Commodus were also much occupied defeating the Sarmatians, which might be an explanation were it not for the fact that these Sarmatians were no longer in Central Asia but the upper Balkans. Moreover, this renewed interest in the east led to the emperors themselves, from Trajan on, again seeing themselves as *neoi Dionysoi*, 'new Dionysoses', so the god returns to favour along with the trappings of his triumphs. On the Beneventum triumphal arch (dedicated in AD 114) Dionysos/Bacchus/Liber are restored to some prominence, although we have no detailed record of the appearance of an imperial Dionysiac triumph of the period. However, Elagabalus (reigned AD 218-22) dressed as Dionysos for a triumph, and later emperors included elephant chariots in their triumphal processions. On a medallion of Marcus Aurelius the young Dionysos is himself elevated on a chariot drawn by musical centaurs with an Eros on their backs and satyrs attending,[20] and the old themes are being revived.

The composition of the scenes on the sarcophagi for the most part includes generic statements of a victory celebration of the type already made familiar on the cameos, and including many other of the by then familiar Dionysiac groups involving drunken Silenos with or without his donkey, maenads, Ariadne and others.

The foreign elements may owe something to such special events as the tradition of the Ptolemaic procession. Thus, on one fragment we have an

---

[19] Important discussion and references in G. Koch and H. Sichtermann, *Römische Sarkophage* (Munich, 1982) 191-5, and Turcan (a rather diffuse but well-illustrated study). Full publication in Matz. Also F. Matz, *Der Gott auf dem Elefantenwagen* (Wiesbaden, 1952) for relationship also with Apollo as a light-god. And see P. Zanker and B.C.Ewald, *Mit Mythen leben* (Munich, 2004) 135-54.
[20] *LIMC* III, pl. 451, no. 224a.

elephant, and in front a flat cart carrying only a massive wine vase, and drawn by lions, such as appeared in the Alexandria procession.[21] But for the most part the indications of a foreign triumph are defined by, for instance, the presence of lions, panthers or elephants, often drawing the chariots/carts. There would be nothing much to identify the triumph as a military one but for a very few examples where fighting is involved and Indians are shown – these are exceptional and for the most part the blood-letting aspects of the triumph are not conspicuous at all, and probably not meant to be called to mind by any viewer, for whom the triumph of the god in the traditional form and with traditional behaviour was enough, without any recollection of or allusion to fighting rather than drinking.

The principal elements are easily defined. The vehicles are rarely at all like real chariots, except where they are made to look like a wheeled throne with the passenger commonly facing backwards. Many are the Bath-chair type as on the cameos, or simply flat platforms on two or four wheels. These had already been devised for the late Hellenistic cameos. The occupant may be the god himself, usually young, very rarely old, and he may be accompanied by Ariadne, seated on his lap – or him on hers, or a satyr. Sometimes they stand.

Occasionally another deity in a chariot may attend – Aphrodite, for example, her lion team led by Eros, who may also be prominent where Dionysos and Ariadne are shown and the love element is apparent. Where Eros leads a lion team he resembles the cameo Eros [fig. 15] and he often rides a lion. The animals pulling the vehicles are seldom horses, more often centaurs (old and young, male, and female), carrying cups or musical instruments, or felines, sometimes elephants, and the team may be led by satyrs or occasionally Eros.[22] An inappropriate African giraffe may appear too, or, more properly, a camel, but not a real two-humped Bactrian, as well as monkeys and all types of feline. African creatures were, after all, more familiar and readily available for display in Italy than eastern ones. Once an elephant carries a whole carousal group in the howdah on his back [fig. 16].[23] Other unusual loads include a party of men around a large pot,[24] and a collection of trophy arms, again with a large pot [fig. 17].[25]

The god may simply be carried on a lion's back in abridged scenes, losing the processional aspect thereby. He often appeared thus in the Hellenistic period,

---

[21] Turcan, pl. 16b (Private, once Palazzo Mattei, Rome).
[22] Notably on a Munich sarcophagus where he is in the pose of the earlier cameo [fig. 15]: Turcan, pl. 11a.
[23] Turcan, pl. 5a (Cambridge); Matz II, pl. 153, no. 129.
[24] Matz II, pl. 156, no. 134 (Rome, Villa Albani).
[25] Matz II, pl. 166, no. 135 (Frankfurt).

Figure 16: Sarcophagus. Once Rome, Palazzo Mattei.

Figure 17: Sarcophagus. Frankfurt, Liebighaus.

Figure 18:Sarcophagus. Rome, Conservatori.

notably on mosaics, without further military connotations but alluding to his eastern associations. Old Silenos, collapsed on his donkey or being supported by satyrs, even sometimes in a chariot/cart, is the most prominent extra, along with Pan. The satyrs are usually involved in something bibulous or musical or may carry trays of fruit. Maenads dance or contribute to the music (pipes, cymbals). Once a small chariot is added to carry two drunken maenads [fig. 18].[26] An unusual addition may be armed Amazon figures, implying their support of the god rather than their Central Asian kin.[27]

The Indian enemy is not often made explicit. Some are shown as captives, youths with long corkscrew curls.[28] Elsewhere some fighting goes on in a limited way.[29]

---

[26] Matz II, pl. 168.2, no. 152; E. la Rocca and S.Tortorella, *Trionfi romani* (2008) 115.
[27] Turcan, pl. 58a,c (Paris).
[28] Turcan, pl. 33a (Florence, Uffizi); Matz II, pl. 135, no. 115.(Florence, Uffizi); pl. 158, no. 130 (Roma, Villa Medici); pl. 161, no. 137 (Vatican, Belvedere).
[29] Turcan, pl. 35 (Lyon); Matz III, nos. 237-45.

Figure 19: Sarcophagus. Boston, Museum of Fine Arts 1972.650.

Where the cortège approaches a sleeping Ariadne we are on Naxos, and only the trappings of the god's team suggest that this could be taken as an extension or welcome goal of his Indian triumph. Otherwise location is not defined, but one is reminded of the roaring buried elephants on Samos, remains of Dionysos' return from fighting the Amazons in the east – in fact a brave interpretation of uncovered fossils.[30] In foot processions Apollo and other deities may attend,[31] Herakles may even share Dionysos' chariot;[32] he is often drunken[33] and may also bear a long torch, like a satyr.[34] Elephant-riders may be Eros, a satyr, or the defeated Indians themselves.[35]

Other Dionysiac allusions abound – some to initiation and divination (a *liknon* winnowing basket, and a round basket with snake emerging), which may have seemed appropriate to what was after all a funeral monument with connotations of immortality, as well as theatrical masks for the God of Theatre.

One or two of the more splendid of the sarcophagi deserve closer descriptions to demonstrate the style and some of the attendant figures just noted – one in

---

[30] J. Boardman, *The Archaeology of Nostalgia* (London, 2002) 42.
[31] Turcan, pl. 37a (Rome, Torlonia).
[32] Turcan, pl. 36c (Vatican, Chiaramonti); Matz II, pl. 167, no. 160.
[33] Turcan, pl. 35 (Lyon).
[34] Matz II, pl. 121, no. 98; 124, no. 99.
[35] E.g., our [fig. 20].

Boston [fig. 19].³⁶ Dionysos and Ariadne stand in a real chariot, looking round. The chariot is drawn by two elephants, ridden by Erotes, one of whom also looks round, while the other pulls the hair of an old man who is holding on his shoulders a wine crater being investigated by two monkeys. Panthers gambol at their feet. A standing naked youth is with another man, one maenad, and another behind with a torch (?) raised in her hand. Beside her is a woman carrying a *liknon* basket, a reference to initiation, and in the foreground an old man tends to a lion, beneath which is a male head/mask, with a giraffe beyond. On the ground a baby crouches before a box from which a snake emerges, another initiatory symbol. There is then a rout of Pan, women and youths, playing cymbals and pipes, led by a dancing satyr holding an animal skin. Beside him on the ground is a small altar with a cup on it, and a crouching child tending a kid. At the right three satyrs support a drunken Herakles, whose club one of them holds, a bowl on the ground. He lurches towards a near-naked woman who shrinks from him; a tree beyond. The mixture of motifs is instructive. From the left the traditional procession develops with strong oriental elements but including the figure of a prominent youth; then a more traditional Dionysiac rout, with intimations of initiation such as are appropriate for a sarcophagus, culminating in a traditional group of drunken Herakles and a woman threatened (Omphale?).

The presence of the drunken Herakles in the Dionysiac rout that may accompany the procession is worth noting, especially in view of the hero's eastern associations (his figure was borrowed for eastern divine figures – Verethagna, Vajrapani, and a site for his rescue of Prometheus was even found in the Hindu Kush), quite apart from his easy relationship with the most relaxed of the Olympians. He demonstrates the effect of Dionysos (wine) on even the immortal.³⁷

A most intricate example at Woburn Abbey presents one of the more populous and elaborated versions of the procession [fig. 20].³⁸ It is much restored but the details of the main figures are readily discerned. A fully dressed Dionysos stands in a normal but highly decorated chariot holding a thyrsos and a strap attached to the yoke of a tiger and tigress which pull it. On their backs sit two small Indian (corkscrew curls) grooms, holding a torch and a harp (?), and below them a baby satyr plays with a goat. Attending the god, behind, are a dancing maenad holding a trophy (?) whose top is missing (in the corner, restored as a hook), and a young satyr, in the chariot, wearing an animal skin

---

[36] Boston, MFA 1972.650; *LIMC* Suppl. 2009, 187, no. add36, pl. 94. Not in Matz.
[37] Herakles and Dionysos: see *LIMC* V, 154-60.
[38] Matz II, pl. 126, no. 100. E. Angelicoussis, *The Woburn Abbey Collection of Classical Antiquities* (Mainz, 1992), no. 62; for the fullest description. Dated to the 220s AD.

Figure 20: Sarcophagus. Woburn Abbey.

and holding a throwing stick (*pedum*). Before the god a Victory is crowning him, and a woman holds a lamp; and behind Victory a maenad pipes. A full-grown Pan with animal ears and feet leads the tigers by a strap attached to the yoke, and a smaller Pan with animal legs, holding a horn or throwing stick and *syrinx* (Pan-pipes). His foot is on a ram's head behind which is a lidded basket (its snake missing), beyond which is another ram's head and snake (?).

Above him, at the top, a child is riding a camel of which we have just the head and neck, a satyr head before it. But behind him is a great elephant ridden by a bound Indian with corkscrew curls. Behind him and before him, at the top, are the heads of two other Indians, the head of a giraffe (not an Indian creature) behind them. The whole Indian rests his elbow on a pot. Below the elephant is a naked Pan with a throwing stick and a lion, while the beast is trampling a lioness or panther, beyond which is another small Indian. Then a new chariot appears with a sober Herakles standing in it, naked but for a knotted sash, and holding a kantharos cup and his club and lionskin. The chariot is drawn by a lyre-playing centaur and a centauress, playing a tambourine. Below are a young satyr with a stick riding a panther, a satyr mask, a panther, a baby holding a cup and stick, and a tiny female in the corner. Higher, to the right of Herakles, an old satyr adjusts his wreath and a man (a mountain god?) is seated holding a frond. Finally, a herm (much

THE PROCESSION IN HELLENISTIC AND ROMAN ART AND LIFE

Figure 21: Silver handle. New York, Met.Mus.

Figure 22: Silver bowl. Washington, Dumbarton Oaks.

restored) set on a wreathed pillar. Very few of these reliefs closely repeat their compositions, and the genre offers perhaps the greatest originality of choice in the whole series of Roman sarcophagi.

This late in the Roman period it is only these sarcophagi that present regular and in their way canonical views of the procession, with all or many of the appropriate figures. The subject, however, proliferates in the other arts although seldom with the same degree of detail. Sometimes we see just the god's chariot and at best the usual accompanying figures and animals.

In the second century AD on a Roman silver handle in New York the god's pard chariot is accompanied by a Pan and a man carrying a large bull's head on his shoulders [fig. 21],[39] and, more in the spirit of the sarcophagi, there is a larger group on a silver bowl in Washington, perhaps 4th-century in date [fig. 22]. On this we have also a drunken Herakles in attendance.[40] The feline, elephant and centaur teams are also borrowed to pull the chariots of others, even mortal emperors, as we have seen.

Mosaics

Paintings depicting the triumph are not known from early centuries AD, and at any rate there are few surviving, although we might have expected something from Pompeii or Herculaneum (but then before the period of the sarcophagi). Philostratus describes a painting of Dionysos and Ariadne with a leopard just appearing, but on a sober occasion (*Imag.* 1.15) and Callistratus a statue of a reclining drunken Indian (*Descr.* 4). So we have to turn to the only related major medium for the subject in the Roman period, beside the sarcophagi, which is mosaic. Here it is plentiful, since this was a subject particularly suited to the decoration of villas, dining rooms and public buildings, where a degree of festivity might be expected and called for an appropriate divine commentary in the decor.

The compositions are not generally as ambitious as those on the sarcophagi, a matter dictated by space available, and they very often seem to depend on particular models which are copied or adapted in different areas of the empire. Thus, in North Africa, it has been thought that the scenes owed much to the relief shown on the Maison d'Arsenal at Sousse, a major Roman site.[41] The god is usually in an ordinary chariot, drawn by centaurs or felines, and is accompanied

---

[39] Ettinghausen, pl. 7.24. In New York. C. Alexander, *Met.Mus.Bulletin* 14.3 (1955) 64-7.
[40] In Washington, Ettinghausen, pl. 4.11.
[41] For the North African mosaics see K.M. Dunbabin, *The Mosaics of Roman North Africa* (Oxford, 1978) 181-2 and her detailed article in *Papers of the British School at Rome* 39 (1971) 52-65.

Figure 23: Mosaic. Sousse, House of Virgil.

by Victory, with the usual rout of satyrs and maenads but nothing more elaborate iconographically. In the House of Virgil at Sousse [fig. 23] the god has Victory beside him in the chariot drawn by tigers, and below them a feline drinks from an open crater, an isolated motif which is relatively rare, but which appears in subsidiary positions on sarcophagi and will be remembered in the east.[42]

At El Djem the unusual vehicle is a sarcophagus-like box with decorated side panels, a favourite carriage in such scenes in the area, but generally undecorated.[43] But at El Djem too we get the engaging addition of Silenos sprawled on a camel,

---

[42] C. Kondoleon, *Domestic and Divine* (Cornell, 1995) 241, fig. 152; ibid., 197, fig. 121, for the Nike beside the god also on a mosaic at Setif (Algeria).
[43] Dunbabin, op.cit., (1978), pl. 71.182.

Figure 24: Mosaic. Cyprus, Nea Paphos, House of Dionysos.

not a donkey.[44] In Portugal, Torre de Palma, the accompanying group of figures is more static, marionettish.[45]

The North African scheme seems to have been followed also in the east, at Antioch, with the god in a frontal tiger chariot, Ariadne standing beside him, the cista, a maenad and Pan.[46] The frontal chariot is going to be an important new presentation of the subject, abandoning the processional.

The mid-second century AD House of Dionysos at Nea Paphos in Cyprus won its name from a mosaic floor which included an 'Invention of Wine' panel, and a triumph, or rather a select view of the triumph in a static mode.[47] Centrally

---

[44] Kondoleon, op.cit., 199, fig. 123.
[45] Kondoleon, op.cit., 210, fig. 135. On the theme on mosaics in Spain see G. Lopez Monteagudo in *Assaph* 4 (1999: Studies in art history of the theatre) 35-60.
[46] D. Levi, *Antioch Mosaic Pavements* (Princeton, 1947) pl. 16c.
[47] Kondoleon, op.cit., fig. 120; ch. 6 for a full description and commentary.

the god stands in his chariot drawn by leopards and attended by Silenos, while a satyr with wineskin and crater steps on to the chariot [fig. 24]. To left and right are maenads, Pan, and two bound male captives with a kneeling prisoner offering a sack who show that this is an after-battle event. One feels that the artist has made a not quite arbitrary selection of subjects from a larger repertoire, and presented it statically, to create an agreeably symmetrical image for the floor space. A simpler but more canonical mosaic floor in another Paphian house (of Aion) has male and female centaurs drawing the chariot, Silenos on a donkey, and a maenad carrying a long conical sacral object.[48]

The Late Roman world and Byzantium

The later antique, Christian world, did not forget its iconographic heritage of paganism but often re-interpreted it, and Dionysos could even hold promise of immortality. Where a Dionysos/Bacchus was to be figured he could easily be shown in a triumphal mood, even if it is indicated simply by his chariot.[49] Egypt and the east generally is now again a prominent source of images and the triumph may be more fully rendered again. An ivory box in Vienna has a warlike Dionysos, with torch and shield, in a panther chariot trampling Indians [fig. 25].[50]

Figure 25: Ivory box. Vienna, Kunsthist.Mus. X 41.

---

[48] Kondoleon, op.cit., 199, fig. 124. W.A. Daszewski, *Dionysos der Erlöser* (1985) 24-27.

[49] Thus, in a centaur chariot on a 4th/5th century marble table in Vienna: *Revue .Archéologique*. 1995, 325-6, fig.

[50] H. Peirce and R. Tyler, *L'Art Byzantin* II (1934) pl. 158c; *LIMC* III, pl. 417, no. 126; W.F. Vollbach, *Elfenbeinarbeiten der Spätantike und des frühen Mittelalters* (Mainz 1976) pl. 54.100, and cf. pl. 52.95 (Bologna; Peirce and Tyler, op. cit., I, no. 160a,b).

Figure 26: Ivory box. New York, Met.Mus.

Another, in New York [fig. 26], is more detailed: the god seems to have a club and quiver, his panthers crush an Indian, with a Pan beyond; the god again, perhaps, attacks other Indians helped by an archer, then a real Pan joins the battle and a masked (?) old man holds a flail.[51] The composition is incoherent but forceful.

On late antique textiles in Egypt, a major source of classical iconography, the groups becomes more heraldic, with the god in a frontal chariot drawn by panthers or centaurs, often with Ariadne, and the Indian element eliminated but for occasional bound figures. Textiles in St Petersburg and New York offer the basic scheme: Dionysos wears a turreted crown, which may be a deliberately eastern feature for a trimphant leader, and he stands on his frontal chariot pulled by two panthers; in New York he is attended by a satyr, two maenads and a bound Indian; in St Petersburg by Pan, two maenads, and a similar bound Indian [fig. 27].[52]

The many simpler scenes on Coptic textiles present just the frontal chariot with panthers or centaurs, and seldom much more [fig. 28].[53] The strongly frontal aspect of the scenes may itself be more than an accidental reflection of the preferred composition of narrative scenes in the east, as

---

[51] Peirce and Tyler, op.cit., II, no. 160a.
[52] Peirce and Tyler, op.cit., II, nos. 133-136a. V.F. Lenzen, 'The Triumph of Dionysos on Textiles of Late Antique Egypt' (*Univ.Calif.Publ.Class.Arch.* 5.1, 1-38, 1960).
[53] Bonhams, London, 28.4.2010, lot 348, with musical centaurs.

Figure 27: Textile. St. Petersburg, Hermitage.

in Parthian and Sasanian art. And outside the Christian world, in Sasanian Persia, Dionysiac motifs flourish, derived from the past or freshly from the west.[54]

Yet, despite this relative lack of interest on the part of artists, the late Roman/Greek world produced also the most lengthy surviving account of Dionysos, in verse, in the early fifth century AD. The author was Nonnos, who lived in Egypt at Panopolis (an evocative name), and wrote both a paraphrase of St John's Gospel, and an epic *Dionysiaka* in 48 books, the longest Greek poem extant, and in reasonable hexameters although 1200 years after Homer. Panopolis was Egyptian Akhmim, some 400 miles up the Nile, site of the temple of the phallic god Min who was readily equated with the Greek god Pan, and an important source for the late decorated

---

[54] Ettinghausen, ch. 1 (the bronze from the Persian Gulf, pl. 8.26, is surely a Pan with a cartload of putti, not Poseidon).

Figure 28: Textile. London Market.

textiles with so much classical iconography. The poem is, in the words of its Loeb translator W.H.D. Rouse, a 'Niagara of words'. It provides and invents details of Dionysos' life and campaigns in the greatest detail, and his association with wild animals, the expected felines and elephants, but also bears, appears throughout.

The fight with the Indians, which also involves a civil war among the gods, is the dominant theme, yet the triumphal return is more about geography than the trappings of the procession, and is in no way a commentary on the traditional Triumph as known in art, but Ariadne's role in the climax is acknowledged and reflects a growing interest in their relationship. In these respects Nonnos seems almost deliberately to ignore much of the artistic tradition, and there is much in his work which can be closely associated with

Figure 29: Ivory box. The Veroli Casket. London, V&A.

the Christianity of the day, in an area where Christian and pagan iconography can intermingle so freely.[55] Moreover, we lack details and texts for many literary treatments of the god from the 2nd to 5th centuries AD upon which Nonnos may have built.[56]

The later Byzantine world and its artists took a more intimate view of their classical tradition, including its figures and stories. While any Christian application may be hard to detect, the creation of new versions of the old

---

[55] R. Shorrock, *The Myth of Paganism* (Bristol, 2011); rev. *Journal of Hellenic Studies* 132 (2012) 194.
[56] Nonnos is most accessible in the three Loeb volumes with translation by W.H.D. Rouse. See also an important collection of essays: *Studies in the Dionysiaca of Nonnus* (ed. N. Hopkinson, Cambridge Phil. Soc. Suppl. Vol. 17, 1994); for earlier sources AD, ibid., 1-2, 23-9, and 156-64 (G. Bowersock on Dionysos as an epic hero; also in his *Hellenism in Late Antiquity* (1990) ch.4). It has been suggested that some of the Roman emperors, like Septimius Severus, who campaigned in the east and could be shown in elephant chariots, had reawakened the interest in Dionysiac parallels and so helped inspire Nonnos, but this seems unlikely, or at least there is no more explicit evidence for it.

subjects, with a slightly modified cast, anticipates much the same attitude that was to be adopted by artists of the Renaissance.

It often seems that we have not left pagan antiquity behind at all.

A prime example is the ivory 'Veroli casket' in the Victoria and Albert Museum, of about AD 1000, a brilliant European classicising work not much dependent on earlier Coptic Christian traditions. Its mythological subjects may indeed have a common message about astral theology, as has been argued. One panel is a clear statement of a version of our triumphant Dionysos, possibly presented as a sun-god [fig. 29]. He reclines holding a whip ('a misunderstood thyrsos' has been suggested) on a flat wheeled platform drawn by two lions. All other reference to the original setting has been eliminated. It is, it seems, a drunken Eros lost in a basket who occupies the field, where there are otherwise just two trees, but the figural theme of the god in his car was strong enough still to be reproduced unmistakably and the group is not unique in this period.[57]

---

[57] E. Simon, op.cit. (n. 32) 1-65, esp. 48-52. Full publication in J. Beckwith, *The Veroli Casket* (London, V&A, 1962). A similar scene on an ivory in Venice, without the Eros and trees: K. Weitzmann, *Greek Mythology in Byzantine Art* (Princeton, 1951) pl. 43.155; the London relief, pl. 56.229; the Eros in basket appears on the Venice codex (Pseudo-Oppian MS), pl. 39.138.

Chapter V

THE ORIENTAL SUCCESSION

Given the strong eastern connections of the Dionysiac procession in Hellenistic and Roman art it is perhaps surprising that the graecising arts of Asia, in Bactria, Gandara and elsewhere, seem to bear only the slightest trace of it, although there are plenty of broadly Dionysiac subjects, down to the great, though miniature, group in gold relief of Dionysos and Ariadne seated on a lion and being crowned by Victory from mid-first-century AD Tillya Tepe in Bactria [fig. 30], North Afghanistan.[1] This derives from some locally Greek-inspired model and need not relate to any eastern victories of the god over the natives. But the fact that a triumph (seated on a lion and the presence of Victory) seems indicated rather than a marriage (and Ariadne commonly accompanies the god in other triumph scenes), means that the group carries the main messages of the more elaborate scenes in the west. Moreover, Ariadne wears a nomad cap, and nomad sleeves under her Greek dress: she has become naturalised in the east, a new Roxane for Dionysos/Alexander. And the satyr in the bottom corner catching spill from Dionysos' cup in his drinking horn, wears his pelt as a belted coat rather than growing it himself.

Of the many Dionysiac subjects in Gandharan relief art of the early centuries AD little directly reflects the triumph motifs, though we find a very realistic Indian Silenos supported physically and with liquor by women and a man, on his mule, with Indian garlands but Greek dress [fig. 31], as on the arts of the west.[2]

Otherwise, there was no little export of classical silver to the east, even as far as China, and upon it many Dionysiac motifs, though none of the triumph,

---

[1] J. Boardman in *Ancient West and East* 2 (2003) 350-3, and in *Afghanistan* (ed. J. Aruz, 2012) 105-6.
[2] J. Boardman, *The Archaeology of Nostalgia* (2002) 124, fig. 92.

to my knowledge.[3] There were, however, some remarkable echoes of the western processions which must have been available to some eastern artists to copy, possibly from cameos or metalwork. They are a clear indication that the traditional presentation of the triumph was known in the east, even though we have so far found no original examples of it. Moreover, the subject is generally misunderstood, at least in terms of Greek divine identities and behaviour, but the

Figure 30: Gold plaque. Kabul Museum.

Figure 31: Relief. Market.

---

[3] E.g., the cup from China with a Dionysos riding a leopard, bearing a Bactrian/Greek weight inscription (F. Baratte, *Arts asiatiques* 51 (1996) 142-7); and a sacral scene (E. Errington and J. Cribb, eds., *The Crossroads of Asia* (Cambridge, 1992) no. 97); both 1st/2nd century AD. For Dionysiac subjects in Gandharan art see now P. Brancaccio and Xinru Liu in *Journal of Global History* 4.2 (2009) 219-44.

THE ORIENTAL SUCCESSION 47

Figure 32: Gilt silver dish. London, British Museum, WA 124086.

Figure 33: Gilt silver dish. Washington, Freer Gallery, 64.10.

origins are unmistakable. They form an interesting commentary on the survival and reinterpretation of classical themes far from Mediterreanean shores, and, in this case, of a theme with an original eastern setting.

A gilt silver dish had been a prized possession of the rulers of Badakshan in north-eastern Afghanistan, in the 19th century.[4] They sold it and it passed through various hands, Afghan and British, thanks to British activity on the North-west Frontier. In 1846 it was put in the Indian Museum in Calcutta and transferred to the British Museum in 1900 [fig. 32]. Its technique resembles that of Sasanian dishes, but it might well be somewhat earlier than the main Sasanian series, perhaps even as early as the 2nd century AD – Parthian or Kushan; a successor, then, to the Tillya Tepe gold of the 1st century which carried so many echoes of more pure Greco-Bactrian derivation. At any rate, it stands technically at the head of a long and distinctive series of gilt silver

---

[4] This is discussed by me in *Classical Art in Eastern Translation* (17th Myres Memorial Lecture, Leopard's Head Press, Oxford, 1993); and in *The Diffusion of Classical Art in Antiquity* (London, 1994) 94-7. For the Sasanian versions (as our fig. 33) see ibid., and Ettinghausen, 4 (who takes the main figure for a male, Dionysos: he is certainly more fully clad than the women). The askos, fig. 22 in the Myres Lecture, is a forgery – H. Kammerer-Grothaus, *Keramos* 173 (2001) 108-9.

bowls made in the Sasanian world, and like several others, its subject was a version of a classical group. We immediately recognise elements copied from the Dionysiac triumph processions as we know it especially on the Medici and glass cameos [figs. 10, 12] but significantly misunderstood – the pose of the two women, one turning to the other and their arms set as if to be pulling something, but now they are not attached to anything and they are wingless; the original Eros on or around the chariot pole is here holding a jug, and connected to a flying Eros with ribbons overhead, both part of the cameo compositions, as is the Eros busy at the wheel. But the chariot or cart has been turned into a plane top view, a rectangle, like the carpets shown in later eastern art, and on it reclines a Herakles with an eastern handleless cup, not Dionysos. He closely resembles the Herakles/Verethagna figure carved on the cliff at Persian Bisitun,[5] a translated Herakles figure which had a long career as a Parthian and Indian deity. On the corner of the chariot/carpet sits a small dressed woman, a relic of Ariadne or the Psyche on the glass cameo [fig. 12] Behind them, before a vine, skips a burly satyr in the 'Praxitelean' pose very familiar from many early Roman reliefs of Dionysiac revels. He has a tiny goat's tail, long overlooked by scholars who have called him Herakles because he carries a stout throwing stick, rather like a club, and animal skin, as might also any satyr. In the exergue a panther investigates a wine vase, as on several Roman sarcophagi, including those with scenes of the triumph, but here flanked by eastern peonies. Our Dionysiac procession has found a new role and identities, but we may suspect that already the function of the subject and the actions of the figures attending a chariot, have been forgotten or misunderstood, and they now serve a more static festive group.

The scheme of the Badakshan dish was reprised in Sasanian Persia, twice, but with some further change of roles [fig. 33]. The fact that it appears in this Persian setting may suggest more strongly that its model (the Badakshan dish) is Parthian. We may certainly now question whether the scene was still recognised as having anything to do with a chariot, especially since there are now two Erotes busy with the wheel, from opposite sides, and the notion of handling an oriental Wheel of Fate has intervened, rather than assisted locomotion. Moreover, the figure on the carpet-like 'chariot' is now a female goddess, barely dressed and attended by a naked female in the customary position. The two women and the two Erotes at the left are in their traditional poses, but still not attached to anything, while the satyr behind does seem to have become attached to the vine behind him, as a supernatural rustic who needs explanation, but not here. The panther and pot in the exergues

---

[5] The lecture (last note) 20, fig. 19.

now have musician attendants. These dishes, probably no earlier than 5th-century AD, have come a long way in their iconography from the western Dionysiac processions of the turn of the era, but virtually all the elements have been preserved, however translated, for a different people and religion. They indicate that the model had somehow survived in the east to be copied, possibly even from the Badakshan dish itself which may have enjoyed some special religious or 'royal' status in the provinces. It is even possible that the scheme contributed to many later scenes of the convivial, '…a loaf of bread, a jug of wine and thou', with all vestiges of locomotion removed.[6]

The vinous themes of much in Sasanian art quite possibly derive from knowledge and approval of Dionysos. The god himself, with thyrsos and panther, appears on a silver cup.[7] So it is in Sasanian art that we perceive also some of the last vestiges of the classical triumph in the east. The flying Eros with a ribbon from the original group long survives to attend royal figures on triumphal reliefs and on silver plates, also at musical parties and attending the Moon God's chariot of zebus. It has been thought that he had become assimilated to an eastern deity, perhaps Apam-Napât, an Indo-Persian deity of water and perhaps lightning, his identity forgotten and translated into something quite new.[8] But we cannot be sure about this and his role remains as it had often been in the classical world, celebrating successes of various sorts, and here substituting for the classical Nike/Victory, who certainly found a new identity in the east (as an Indian *apsara*, and as far as China).[9] But we must return to Europe.

---

[6] E.g. the London plate, *Mesopotamia and Iran in the Parthian and Sasanian Periods* (ed. J. Curtis, British Museum, 2000) pl. 22. M.M. Kouhpar and T. Taylor make the same observation in D. Kenner and P. Luft (eds.) *Current Research in Sasanian Archaeology* (Oxford. BAR, 2008) 127-35. C. Delacour, *MonumentsPiot* 84 (2005) 65-98, thinks to pursue the motif into China, which seems to me doubtful.
[7] Ettinghausen, pl. 1.1 and cf. 1.2; ch. 1 on such Dionysiac motifs.
[8] A. Soudavar, *Iranica Antiqua* 44 (2009) 1-42, explains and illustrates the new function.
[9] J. Boardman, *The Diffusion of Classical Art in Antiquity* (1994) 151-153.

Chapter VI

THE RENAISSANCE

The later Middle Ages in Christian Europe offer nothing as evocatively classical as could Byzantine art. The mediaeval pageant, involving processions, the carriage of images and a great deal of narrative, was a live enough phenomenon, but the classical subjects, as live models, had been forgotten or were disregarded, and even the classical mode for images of Dionysos/Bacchus and Pan could be forgotten. But the long sleep of classicism came to an end once the original models were recovered, assiduously collected, interpreted or reinterpreted, and copied.

The rebirth of interest in classical arts, the *Rinascimento*, *Renaissance*, was fuelled by the presence, on and in the soil of Italy and of the old Roman Empire, of many surviving examples of statuary and minor objects, notably cameos, and the recovery of yet more by excavation in and around ancient buildings and cemeteries, as well as being abetted by study of ancient texts. An early and very literary reflection of our subject appears in the strange *Hypnerotomachia* published in 1499, a prose epic following the dream progress of one Poliphilo through an imaginary but very classical landscape. The book was heavily illustrated. I show the drawing of the Triumph of Semele [fig. 34],[1] Dionysos' mother. Her son's vine is prominently displayed atop an urn on a variety of the triumphal cart which will be met often in the 15th and 16th centuries.

It is drawn by a team of three pairs of pards, accompanied by naked 'maenad' women carrying various trophies, one at least very like a thyrsos, a

---

[1] J. Godwin, *The Pagan Dream of the Renaissance* (London, 2002) 25, fig. And cf. Jennings, *Parades* 14f.

Figure 34: Drawing from Hypnerotomachia.

classical Silenos rides a donkey and a woman carries on her head a flat basket, copying the *vannus* of the classical scenes. This is the pattern for numerous real and imagined 'joyous entries' and festivals of both earlier and coming years, with similar transport and accompaniment, and of marvellous displays, modelled on what could be learned from antiquity about military triumphs and festivals; thus, in 1443, a triumphal chariot with Alexander the Great standing on a turning world globe, angels, cherubim, unicorns and a self-propelled car.[2] Petrarch's *Rime e triumphi* included the triumph of Dionysos and Ariadne, and the Putti Master engraved an aquatic version.[3]

The closest use of the sarcophagus scenes for a Renaissance triumph is by Perino del Vaga in a painting for a vault in the Villa Doria at Genoa [fig. 35] where we see the Indians, elephants and camels as well as the rout.[4] Other Renaissance uses of the triumphal chariot are legion and without direct reference either to the

---

[2] Godwin, op.cit., 183, and ch. 9 for all such displays.
[3] L. Armstrong, *Renaissance Miniature Painters and Classical Imagery* (London,1981) 51 and ill. 54.
[4] B. Wisch and S.S. Munshowe (eds.), *Art and Pageantry* (Philadelphia, 1990) fig. 5-20. Dürer's man pushing a cart may recall the cupids, ibid., fig. 7- 17, 27.

Figure 35: Painting by Perino del Vaga, Genoa.

god of wine or Roman triumph. I show just one, the reverse of a medal of 1630 for Cardinal Richelieu, with victorious France in the chariot and only an Eros behind to hint at something rather less military and to recall the classical scenes [fig. 36].[5]

Only the late 16th-century artist Etienne Delaune offers a drawing of a triumph based more closely on the sarcophagus scenes.[6]

Of physical sources for the observation and copying of classical subjects the monumental arts, figural and architectural, were the most prominent, but there were minor arts too to be recovered on ancient sites, and a great many minor objects had survived above ground since antiquity incorporated in other works. Many a mediaeval cross, reliquary or bookbinding is embellished by the insertion of ancient gems and cameos, and although

Figure 36: Bronze medal. New York, Met.Mus., 31.33.32.

---

[5] New York, Met.Mus. 31.33.32. By Jean Warin (1606-72), Paris, 1630. M. Jones, *The Art of the Medal* (British Museum, 1979) 79, no. 193.

[6] R. Distelberger, *Die Kunst des Steinschnitts* (Skira, 2002) 179; copied on a glass vessel in Vienna, ibid., 178.

the arts of gem engraving had suffered some decline they were being taken up again readily by artists, including the better artists, and were encouraged by noble collectors whose prestige was enhanced by the art they sponsored, which could be admired in cabinets in their homes or on their persons.

It could make them appear the equals of the rulers of the old Roman Empire. For the narrative arts, the sarcophagi proved an especially rich source of inspiration, but the minor arts of cameo-, coin- and medallion-engraving also revived in a spectacular fashion. Moreover, they could more often be true to their models, in detail and style, since the same techniques and materials were employed and to the same effect, while ancient sculpture was copied or used as inspiration in the form in which it had survived – blank white marble or near-black bronze - with none of the colour that had distinguished the ancient originals. This false view of ancient statuary, as blank, colourless, persisted for centuries, indeed survives today for public monuments. But in the minor arts appearances and techniques remained the same, leading sometimes now to distress over identification of original, copy, or 'modern' original, all apparently in the correct ancient style.

Dionysos' eastern adventure receives only passing mention in Renaissance literature, and the artists' ancient literary sources were limited and devoted mainly to other aspects of the god's birth and life. Writers were well enough aware of Bacchus and his revels but generally did not dwell on them, and their sources too were literary rather than art. In France the god received some attention among the Pléiade poets. Ronsard especially wrote a series of poems dedicated to him in 1550-4, including 'Folatrissime voyage d'Hercueil' and 'Hinne de Bacchus', mainly based on Ovid and Statius, presenting him an 'an expression of man's conflicting passions', but at the same time allowing him to set up camp on the left bank of the River Loire, much to the benefit of the local vintages.[7]

In England, however, at the end of the 17th century, Dryden had not forgotten Alexander and Bacchus in 'Alexander's Feast', although he overlooked Alexander's fate:

> The praise of Bacchus, then, the sweet musician sung;
> Of Bacchus ever fair, and ever young,
> The jolly god in triumph comes;
> Sound the trumpets, beat the drums;
> Flushed with a purple grace
> He shows his honest face;
> Now give the hautboys breath; he comes, he comes.

---

[7] T. Cave in A.H.T. Levi, *Humanism in France* (Manchester, 1970) 249-270: 'The Triumph of Bacchus and its interpretation in the French renaissance'.

Bacchus, ever fair and young,
Drinking joys did first ordain;
Bacchus' blessings are a treasure,
Drinking is the soldier's pleasure;
Rich the treasure,
Sweet the pleasure,
Sweet is pleasure after pain.

Figure 37: Florence, Medici Palace

The popularity of the subject in art depended almost wholly on familiarity with the Roman sarcophagus reliefs, and any new works devoted to the theme dwell usually on the presence of Ariadne, who was regarded as a desirable end-product or goal of the procession, and, for the oriental aspect, on a plethora of appropriate wild animals. The most varied medium for showing the triumph is panel painting, but the chariot types used in the traditional processions find their imitations in vehicles for other occasions, real or

Figure 38: Medallion in Medici Palace, Florence.

imaginary (as they had in antiquity), and depicted in all media, notably on cassoni. But we start with the gems as sources.[8]

Cabinets of gems were collected by the noble families of Italy: the Medici in Florence, the Gonzaga in Mantua, the Farnese in Rome. These were the source of inspiration for court artists, and we shall be spending some time on what they copied or adapted for the new princely world. But they were the inspiration for more than the arts of the gem engraver, and our first new Triumph of Dionysos appears as relief sculpture based on an ancient cameo, its figures somewhat translated from their original identities, although not as much as we have seen the earlier oriental versions to have been.

The upper frieze in the interior of the courtyard of the Medici Palace in Florence was decorated with twelve marble relief tondi [fig. 37], eight of them figural and each based on an ancient model, seven of these being gems, and one copying a sarcophagus scene.

The intention seems to have been more than decorative; and there was a didactic programme, though not too easy for us to unravel today. It meant that subjects could be adjusted in various degrees away from the exact detail of their originals. The tondi were carved in about 1460, after earlier drawings, and the gem subjects are all based on pieces in the Medici collection. The execution appears to be that of the workshop of the artist Donatello, and some believe that they are from his hand. The one that concerns us [fig. 38] is clearly based on the cameo we have already considered [fig. 10]. It is true to the original in most respects, but the figure in the chariot is no longer a near-naked Dionysos, but a dressed woman, and her attendant is a child, not a satyr. The model of a trimphant Dionysos has been supplanted by something

---

[8] In general on Renaissance Dionysos see M. Bull, *The Mirror of the Gods* (London, 2005) ch. 6, esp. 254-7.

Figure 39: a. David by Michelangelo, Florence. b. Detail of Goliath's helmet

more subtle, a female personification, it may be, of Virtue, but in the oddest of settings, which is unmistakably that of the Dionysiac triumph.[9]

This is not, however, Donatello's only contribution to our subject. His famous bronze David in Florence [fig. 39a] stands triumphant over the decapitated head of Goliath. The giant's helmet is still in place, and on it we see in low relief a familiar scene: not a chariot this time but the triumphal cart with the high platform to carry a throne [fig. 39b]. Erotes pull the cart and one is busy at the wheel, as he was on the cameo and the marble relief. On the throne is a gaunt, apparently naked bearded figure, slouching, to whom an Eros seems to be offering what may be a cup. Behind the throne is a pot (wine?) and another Eros holds a parasol over the throne. An Eros stands on a pillar before the chariot holding what may be a cup, while three pull the chariot and there is a jug on the ground before them.

The usual Eros pushes the wheel. Wine, it seems, is important. The comparable scenes have sometimes encouraged scholars to see here a triumph

---

[9] The tondo is well explored by E. Simon in *Schriften zur Kunstgeschichte* (Stuttgart, 2003) 93-7, with the tondo and gem illustrated on pl. 10, and the figures taken to be Virtus and Amor caelestis.

Figure 40: Snuff box. London, V&A Museum, 448-2008

Figure 41: Cameo. D. Content Collection.

of Erotes, even an allusion to the Platonic Ideal of Love,[10] neither of them appropriate to a (defeated) Philistine hero, and totally at variance with what we see on the helmet. The enthroned figure ought to be a Philistine noble, king or god, presented by the artist in a very much less than regal or divine manner, indeed slouching drunkenly, but attended as a Dionysos might have been, and borrowing his iconography just as the marble tondo did, also with a change of identity.

The Medici cameos, and others, provided models for several Renaissance versions. When Francesco Gori came to publish drawings of the gems in Florence in 1731-2 he showed several variants on the common theme: Bacchus and Ariadne riding a pantheress; Ariadne caressing Bacchus on a chariot drawn by musical centaurs; Bacchus in a goat-cart with a satyr and maenad, snake-charming.[11] A 16th-century cameo in St Petersburg has Ariadne alone in a chariot escorted by musician cupids and Pan.[12] A fine Roman 18th-century one, set in an English 19th-century gold snuff-box, offers another variant on the theme with most of the figures in the appropriate poses [fig. 40],[13] including the Cupid, but with a pantheress and panther pulling, and a Pan with horn-trumpet and thyrsos.

---

[10] Cf. L. Schneider in *The Art Bulletin* 55 (1973) 215-6.
[11] F. Gori, *Museum Florentinum* (1831) I pls. 91.6, 92.2, 94.2.
[12] J. Kagan, *Western European Cameos* (Leningrad, 1973) no.34.
[13] *Ancient Gem Engraving* (Fukuoka, 2008; Exhibition Catalogue) no. 367; C. Truman, *The Gilbert Collection* (Los Angeles, 1991) I (1991) no. 42. Victoria and Albert Museum Loan Gilbert 448-2008.

An odder cameo version [fig. 41] is possibly ancient but almost more a parody of the Medici cameo. It shows two Erotes pulling the chariot but still in the old Psychai poses. On the chariot is Silenos reclining on animal skins (a lion and goats?), while over him in the usual pose is Psyche, butterfly-winged, holding a

Figure 42: Impression of sard intaglio. Baltimore, Walters Art Museum 42.1176.

Figure 43: Painting by Titian. London, Nat. Gallery.

Figure 44: Painting by Garofalo. Dresden, Gallery.

thyrsos and a goat-headed drinking horn – a good mixture here of triumph and bacchanalia.[14]

The Ariadne theme favoured by painters appears also in gem engraving, for example an intaglio in Baltimore, once in the Marlborough Collection at Blenheim Palace, which recalls Titian: Theseus' ships are rowing away fast from a forlornly gesticulating Ariadne, while Dionysos approaches in a chariot drawn by Pans [fig. 42].[15]

Other major arts are more informative and original in composition. Ariadne as the goal of the procession, whether accidentally or not, is a constant theme, exemplified in Titian's painting [fig. 43] in the National Gallery, London,

---

[14] M. Henig, *The Content Gems* (Oxford, 1990) no. 120. It has been repaired (gold in chipped edges) which perhaps favours an ancient date.
[15] J. Boardman et al., *The Marlborough Gems* (Oxford, 2009) no. 151.

Figure 45: Painting by Carracci. Rome, Farnese Gallery.

Figure 46: Drawing by Penni. British Museum.

Figure 47: Painting by van Heemskeerk. Vienna, Kunsthist. Mus.

where the young god's rather indefinable and cart-like chariot is drawn by cheetahs, and his followers betray nothing especially eastern otherwise.[16]

Benvenuto Garofalo's 1540 Triumph in Dresden has the god and Ariadne in chariot drawn by leopards while cupids and others sport on elephants and the centrepiece is a drunken Silenos [fig. 44]. Annibale Carracci's Triumph for the Farnese Gallery [fig. 45], in 1597, presented Dionysos and Ariadne, each in a throne-chariot pulled by tigers and goats respectively, and with the familiar rout.[17] Again the triumph and wedding aspects are combined. Only Raphael, in a composition preserved in Penni's drawing in the British Museum, places the chariot drawn by lions with the god and Ariadne in second place to a grand display of elephants swarming with putti and the Dionysiac troupe [fig. 46].[18]

In the north, van Heemskerck's *Triumph* [fig. 47] [19] offers Dionysos more as Silenos on a throne set on a cart drawn by satyrs, and with enough in the incidental detail to recall strongly the ruins of ancient Rome (a marble foot),

---

[16] The cheetahs, W. Tresidder in *Burlington Magazine* 123 (1981) 481-5. The painting was designed for the *camerino* of Alfonso d'Este; cf. J.J. Campbell, *The Cabinet of Eros* (New Haven, 2004) 20.
[17] There is a good copy of the painting on the ceiling of the hall in West Wycombe House, Oxon.
[18] BM 1895.0915.582.
[19] Bull, op.cit., 255-7, fig. 94.

Figure 48: Shell cameo. Boston, Museum of Fine Arts 99.119.

Figure 49: Painting by Rubens. Rotterdam. Mus. Boymans-van Beuningen.

which were a major source for the theme. Also from the north, Germany in the 16th century, is a shell cameo [fig. 48] from the Arundel collection[20] with Dionysos seated on a long cart pulled by oxen, a lion in attendance and a fine rout of satyrs and maenads occupied with wine. The Pan seated at the front of the cart carries a vinous trophy. Early 17th-century Flemish artists tend to offer Dionysos in the traditional way (but with a real Silenos in the rout), with appropriate animals (leopards), and not necessarily an Ariadne.[21]

Poussin was taken by Nonnos and painted Bacchanals for Cardinal Richelieu, but not the triumph as such rather than a Dionysiac procession with the young god in a chariot drawn by centaurs, and, interestingly, a child

Figure 50: Painting by Mantegna. London, The Queen's Collection.

---

[20] Op.cit., n. 107, no. 50.
[21] Thus, Cornelisz Moeyart (the Hague, with a 'modern' soldier in the troop), Frans II Francken, Cornelis de Vos (Madrid).

Figure 51: Panel by Montorsoli. Genoa.

reaching up to one of the wheels, recalling the role of an Eros in ancient art.[22] Rubens' oil sketch [fig. 49] seems canonical but his Bacchus is gross and we might take him for Silenos but that Silenos is there already, on a donkey at the right. The car is drawn by tigers and two Pans, a black and a maenad attend.[23]

Roman military triumphs were rather more to the taste of Italian Renaissance princes, but even in the great series of triumph paintings made by Mantegna for Mantua we find naked children attending, like putti [fig. 50],[24] and this element of classical attendance could well have been inspired by the Dionysiac rather than the martial Roman. The raised throne on a cart in particular becomes an important element in presentations of various divinities and, probably, in life for rulers and notables. These abound in Renaissance art. Thus, the panel by Montorsoli set over the door of Andrea Dorio's palace at Genoa [fig. 51] presents two princes on the familiar cart, drawn by centaurs and with musical Erotes, with the usual one pushing at the wheel.

---

[22] M. Bull, *Burlington Magazine* 137 (1995) 5-11; 140 (1998) 724-38. The procession, in Kansas City. Nelson-Atkins Museum.
[23] *Corpus Rubenianum* Ludwig Burchard IX (1970) pl. 73.
[24] *Andrea Mantegna* (ed. J. Martineau, Olivetti, 1992), pl. 115.

Figure 52: Gilt automaton by Hans Schottheim. Vienna, Kunsthist. Mus.

What is probably the most evocative Renaissance demonstration of a Dionysiac procession, not wholly a triumph but with other attractions, is a gilt automaton made by Hans Schlottheim of Augsburg in about 1605, which moved, had moving figures and played music.[25] It takes the form of a bulky cart decorated with animal and satyr heads and pulled by a satyr with various other demons. On the cart is a bagpipe player and Dionysos seated on a goat. At 52 cm long it must have made an impressive tablepiece [fig. 52].

The decoration of armour is another field for what were deemed to be appropriate representations of triumphs which, in their chariotry, strongly recall the Dionysiac but no more. They are seen on helmets and corselets alongside many other classically inspired scenes, as of Horatius on Tiber bridge, a popular subject for Renaissance rather than ancient artists.

---

[25] Vienna, Kunsthist.Mus.

Chapter VII

THE MODERN WORLD

The neo-Classical artists of the 18th/19th century were as ready as their predecessors to copy the classical models, none less so than the gem-engravers, but they seldom rise to anything beyond a straight copy or pastiche. There is one exception, the engraver Lorenz Natter, who visited England intending to publish a *Museum Britannicum* of his drawings of the gem collections in Britain, which he judged to be among the best in Europe. He got a long way with this but gave up when he found not much enthusiasm, i.e., backing, for the project, and translating pencil drawings into engravings was expensive. His papers are now in St Petersburg[1] and among them is a drawing of a creation of his own, on a five-layered cameo, the whereabouts of which is unknown (to me, at least). It was based on the Medici cameo but improved [fig. 53].

The naked couple recline on the chaise-chariot but there is a figure behind them holding a lionskin over them. The chariot is drawn by two lions, attended by an Eros seen in back view. Beyond is a woman carrying a tray of fruits and in front, a herm (?). Natter signs below: L.N. This renaissance of the subject had no serious following beyond copies of the old basic group and with no interesting triumphal trimmings.

---

[1] They will be published in a collaborative venture by the Beazley Archive and the Hermitage Museum.

Figure 53: Drawing of a gem by Lorenz Natter.

By the nineteenth century the subject had not been entirely downgraded. Keats, pursuing his nightingale, eschews the opportunity for a more ethereal mount:

> Away, away, for I will fly to thee,
> Not charioted by Bacchus and his pards,
> But on the viewless wings of Poesy
> Though the dull brain perplexes and retards.

However, the poet's Grecian Urn shows him not insensitive to classical models in the arts, and in Endymion the song of the (appropriately) Indian Maid is unequivocally in the full tradition:

The earnest trumpet spake, and silver thrills
From kissing cymbals made a merry din -
Twas Bacchus and his kin!
...
Within his car, aloft, young Bacchus stood,
Trifling his silver dart, in dancing mood,
With sidelong laughing.
...
And near him rode Silenus on his ass,
Pelted with flowers as he on did pass
Tipsily quaffing
...
Onward the tiger and the leopard pants,
With Asian elephants;
...
Mounted on panthers' furs and lions' manes,
From rear to van they scour about the plains.

Figure 54: Silver vase by Paul Storr. London, V&A.

Figure 55: Plaque by Wedgwood.

Nor were the visual arts altogether forgotten. Neoclassical models, preserving the old cameo groups, recur more impressively in silverwork, as by Paul Storr (1771-1844), leading silversmith of the period in England. He used the Eros and chariot group [fig. 54],[2] copied from cameos, on various shapes, as well as more formal versions of Roman triumphs with little or no concessions to the divine.

On the whole, however, the neo-Classical was more attracted to Venus and Cupids than Dionysos/Bacchus, though there are exceptions which go beyond the copying of Storr.

Wedgwood produced a relatively large plaque which combined elements of the triumph but had lost its purpose [fig. 55]: Dionysos with a thyrsos and Ariadne with a jug sit in a Bath-chair drawn by pards and are crowned by Nike. Behind them is a rustic scene of a woman, child and goat, before them a Fortuna and two satyrs with a vine and jug. There are many other Wedgwood variants and reductions of the theme: for instance one in which the Cupid

---

[2] V&A Museum.

Figure 56: Plate by Wedgwood.

Figure 57: Mirror top. Market.

pushes the whole chariot, not just the wheel, ridden by other Cupids and drawn by lions [fig. 56].[3]

An early-19th century mirror top offers a similar restatement of the old themes, with similar misunderstandings of purpose to Wedgwood's [fig. 57].[4] At the right a regular Roman triumphal chariot attended by soldiers, but also by a putto, and drawn by two pairs of lions with two trumpeting Victories overhead. At the left we seem to have the woman with the sacred cista and snake issuing from it, but the snake has turned into a sickle and the whole scene, with drinking, harvesting and fighting putti, takes on a more rustic mode. Delacroix was more conventional with his pard-drawn Dionysos, yet with a tambourine-beating Eros by his wheel.[5] By the end of the century the shell cameo-cutters of Naples were still producing whole Triton shells carved with versions of triumphs which combined almost every possible aspect of the tradition adjusted for the new classical taste, if somewhat incoherent.

In the twentieth century the true classical imagery of the Triumph was not altogether forgotten by artists but depended more closely on the old tradition. At least, Salvador Dali's tribute to the subject does not conceal many of the original elements [fig. 58] and is based on the sarcophagus scenes. The chariot is more like a basis, the god collapsed onto a sheep, the attendants seem to reflect centaurs and Pan, while the chariot is properly drawn by two seriously adjusted elephants. And Mark Antony at last got his lion chariot, figured in the big bronze group made by Arthur Strasser in 1898 [fig. 8]. In literature there seems little. The 'Keats of Kentucky', Madison Julius Cawein (1865-1914), said to have influenced T.S. Eliot, hymned him:

> O, pard-drawn youth, thou didst awake the world
> To joy and pleasure with thy sunny wine!
> Mad'st India bow and the dun, flooding Nile
> Grow purple in the radiance of the wine...

---

[3] The floral groundline is borrowed from Wedgwood's version of the famous Cupid and Psyche cameo: J. Boardman et al., *The Marlborough Gems* (Oxford, 2009) no. 1, with ills., p. 33. Otherwise, Wedgwood has a Bacchus with Pan in a horse-drawn chariot with Eros atop, and the Eros with lions of the cameo [fig. 15]: E.B. Adams, *The Beeson Collection* (Birmingham. Alabama, 1992) nos. 250, 877.
[4] Bonhams, Oxford, 30.3.2011.
[5] Painting in the Stiftung F.G. Bührle, Zurich. L. Johnson, *The Paintings of Delacroix* (Oxford, 1986) no. 253, pl. 71.

Figure 58: Print design by Salvador Dali, 1953.

Better, James Elroy Flecker, who showed us the Golden Road to Samarkand, envisioned an English triumph:

> From Heaven's Gate to Hampstead Heath
> Young Bacchus and his crew
> Came tumbling down, and o'er the town
> Their bursting trumpets blew.
> …..
> From London's houses, huts and flats,
> Came busmen, snobs and Earls,
> And ugly men in bowler hats
> With charming little girls.
> …..
> Far in a rosy mist withdrawn
> The God and all his crew,

> Silenus pulled by nymphs, a faun,
> A satyr drenched in dew.[6]

And, from the sublime ... the pop group Crash Test Dummies issued an album in 1993, 'God shuffled his feet', the cover for which was Titian's painting with the heads replaced by portraits of the performers, and omitting Ariadne.[7]

For processions which seem to recapture, deliberately or not, those of antiquity and the Renaissance, the only candidates in the modern world are provided by the circus. Other parades tend to be purely military, however splendid – in London, the Trooping of the Colour; or domestic – The Lord Mayor's Show, May Day in Washington; or trivial – open-top buses for successful football teams. The 2010 Lord Mayor's Show in London did run to 137 items and floats, but no wild animals.

It would be premature to argue any direct or deliberate association between the Dionysiac Triumph and the modern circus parade, at least on the evidence available, but there are elements that link them quite closely, and there is no denying the comparable composition and spirit of the parades. It would not surprise me if some positive connection should at some time be uncovered, evidence that there was some degree of deliberate revival of classical behaviour. At the least it demonstrates the human interest in processional entertainment, in the display of wild animals associated with ribaldry, and if there is more than a superficial connection between the ringmaster and Dionysos, the circus clown and a satyr, or the women snake-charmers and maenads, at least they demonstrate common human invention in the creation of celebratory public displays, and with a closely comparable choice of participants. It is not impossible that the fashion for travelling menageries, which were more serious and began at about the same time as the circus parades, had some influence on the latter's creation and popularity.[8]

The circus parades began in late 18th century Britain, spreading to Ireland and Europe, with a tradition of having a parade for the circus' arrival in town. The first American circus was set up by an Englishman, Ricketts, in Philadelphia in 1793. Edwin Hughes, manager of Batty's Circus in London, staged an equestrian parade in 1843, including gilded coaches pulled by

---

[6] 'The Ballad of Hampstead Heath'.
[7] It reached no. 9 in the US charts, no. 2 in the UK.
[8] On the travelling menageries see H. Cowie, *Journal of the History of Collections* 25 (2013) 103-117. In 1793 a live hunt was staged in the Theatre Royal, Drury Lane, with 12 hounds, many horsemen and a real fox, preceded by a Grand Equestrian Parade.

elephants and camels, led by an elaborately dressed Hughes in 'The Burmese Imperial State Carriage' drawn by elephants. 'Lord' George Sanger became a millionaire on the business and staged Royal Command performances for Queen Victoria.

Hughes had sold his 'chariots' (an evocative description) to America in 1847, and thereafter the most spectacular continuing history of the genre is enacted in the USA, with Barnum and Bailey, then their successors, the Ringling Brothers. The parade into town often included various classical themes, as well as the general atmosphere of jollity and celebration, of relevance to no particular deity beyond the owner, but intoxicating for the crowd. However, many elements seem very familiar. Exotic animals were and are especial features, elephants and the more dangerous cats, and floats depicting in images, models and dressed performers, some topics of popular interest including military victories. The name itself – circus – throws back to the Roman buildings which had been designed for such displays, accompanying real military triumphs, but also wild-animal displays, and more bloodthirsty spectacles to please the populace. To all these the Dionysiac tradition made and makes its contribution, and in this respect the circus parades seem true descendants of the ancient Dionysiac triumphs.

There was a special effort by the Ringling brothers in 1895 to ward off rivals: 'Three days before the opening, the show moved in a three-mile-long torch-light parade proudly led by Al Ringling on horseback, through the narrow pack-jammed streets of Chicago... There were a fifty-five-piece band; several hundred horses ridden by performers or drawing the red-and-gold chariots; and the cages containing lions and tigers, panthers and pumas, a hippopotamus, a rhinoceros.....Open glass-walled dens displayed snake-charmers working boa constrictors...... Of course, there was a whole herd of elephants, dozens of clowns, and, bringing up the rear, a perfectly deafening musical 'calliope' (a name derived from the Greek Muse and applied to sets of steam-whistles). The nine Landaures in their Living Statue act: 'These ladies and gentlemen, dressed in nothing but very tight tights covered with white paint, assumed the attitudes of famous pieces of classic sculpture'.[9] In this respect at least the classical heritage was acknowledged, while clowns perform as satyrs and snake-charmers as maenads. Hellenistic Alexandrians would have appreciated and understood the show.

Only a slightly different approach was used for the pre-Mardi Gras carnivals in New Orleans. In the 1890s a drawing shows a procession of model animal chariots attended by a plump Silenos on a donkey and a piping Pan [fig.

---

[9] H. Ringling North and A. Hatch, *The Circus Kings* (New York, 1960) 113-4.

Figure 59: Drawing, 1890. New Orleans.

59].[10] The Dionysiac was not forgotten and has indeed been reinstated there in recent years by the formation of a 'Krewe of Bacchus', with appropriate festivities and balls, though antiquity has been rather dismissed in favour of new interpretations, even of Bacchus as a pirate [fig. 60]. In Britain, Gifford's Circus in Oxfordshire still (2013) properly includes a Pan, but as acrobat, not piper [fig. 61].[11]

The tradition lingers but, since World War II, the animal element in circuses has been considerably diluted by considerations of Animal Rights and the like. Nevertheless the spirit lives on especially in the United States, where a whole new organisation for circus parades, if not the circus itself, has grown up in recent years, with clubs, reunions, publications and displays which are by no means diminished in scale. The Great Circus Parade in Milwaukee in 2009

---

[10] Jennings, *Parades* 24, fig. 'The Mystic Krewe of Comus'.
[11] For Pan's survival in the modern world see J. Boardman, *The Great God Pan* (London, 1997) 7-26.

Figure 60: Poster, 2013. New Orleans.   *Figure 61: Gifford's Circus, 2013, Oxfordshire.*

comprised 126 items. There were wild animals, though not as many as there had been years before – tigers (including white), elephants, lions, giraffes, a tapir, kangaroos; snake charmers; clowns; tableaux for fantasy – Cinderella, Mother Goose, Snow White; and for history – Uncle Sam on stilts, Buffalo Bill; the ranch, stage-coachs, covered wagons; plenty of riders and carriages, antique motors, high-wheel cyclists; plenty of music – a Bandwagon pulled by ten horses; the foreign (exotic) – English, Polish, French, Irish, Arabian, Mexican were admitted; finally, those 'Magnificent Street Sweepers of the Milwaukee Sanitation Department'.

The spirit may be the same but the robust detail probably diminished for a more self-conscious and cautious modern world. The last of the great Ringling family parades had taken place in Boston. Only weeks before the death of the last of the New Dionysoses, John Ringling, in 1936, his nephew took him to a parade in Pensacola – I paraphrase the description he gave:[12]

---

[12] Ringling North and Hatch (op.cit.), 235-8. In 1959 Ringling's descendants revived the old parade tradition in 'Circus World'.

[Versions of parts of this essay were delivered in lectures in New York (2003) and Jerusalem (2013), in honour of Elie Borowski.]

'I saw the eight horses with nodding plumes of the band wagon round the corner. Then the full blast of sound hit us, the gay, raucous blare of brass playing circus music. It got louder and behind the tootling musicians I could see red-and-gold howdahs rolling and pitching on the stately gray backs of the elephants. There went the ferocious, man-eating hyenas, the dusty brown bear, and the glowering bald eagle; elk, lions, monkeys, a deer; Aunt Louise wrapped in a boa constrictor; and, very proudly, Babylon and Fannie, those first ponderous pachyderms. A multi-team hitch of horses that filled the whole thoroughfare from curb to curb, pulling a crimson-and-gold wagon as long as a railroad car with thirty musicians playing for dear life. A herd of forty elephants in gorgeous trappings with gorgeous girls on their backs. Another stream of horses drew the Bell Wagon, its carillon chiming sweetly after the noise of the band. Clowns cavorted along, cage after cage of sleek, pacing jungle beasts were followed by the open dens with tamer creatures – Louise the hippo, and Katy, bowing her long reticulate head. Then, blasting us with its cacophony until the buildings seemed to rock, came the biggest steam calliope of them all.

Uncle John was sitting motionless in his chair and tears were streaming like miniature cascades from his eyes. He pushed himself out of his chair with enormous difficulty, and clung to my shoulder. "Time to go home, Buddy," he said.'

Abbreviations

Boardman, *Nostalgia*: J. Boardman, *The Archaeology of Nostalgia* (London, 2002)

Ettinghausen: R. Ettinghausen, *From Byzantium to Sasanian Iran and the Islamic World* (Leiden, 1972).

Jennings, *Parades* : G. Jennings, *Parades. Celebrations and Circuses on the March* (Philadelphia/New York, 1966)

LIMC: *Lexicon Iconographicum Mythologiae Classicae* (Artemis Verlag, 1981-2007)

Matz: C. Robert, G. Rodenwaldt, F. Matz, *Die antiken Sarkophagreliefs* (Berlin 1890-).

ThesCRA : *Thesaurus Cultus et Rituum Antiquorum* (Los Angeles, 2004-12)

Turcan: R. Turcan, *Les Sarcophages romains à représentations dionysiaques* (Paris, 1966)

Vollenweider, *Steinschneidekunst* : M.L. Vollenweider, *Die Steinschneidekunst und ihre Künstler in spätrepublikanischer Zeit* (Baden-Baden, 1963)

Walters: H.B. Walters, *Catalogue of the engraved gems and cameos in the British Museum* (London, 1926)